Advanced Korean

Written by
Jaemin Roh

Edited by
Suzanne McQuade and Sunhee Her

Published in the United States by Living Language, an imprint of Random House, Inc.

www.livinglanguage.com

Editor: Suzanne McQuade
Production Editor: Ciara Robinson
Production Manager: Tom Marshall
Interior Design: Sophie Chin
Production Design: Ann McBride
Illustrations: Sophie Chin
Audio Producer: Ok Hee Kolwitz

First Edition

ISBN: 978-0-307-97223-1

This book is available at special discounts for bulk purchases for sales promotions or premiums. Special editions, including personalized covers, excerpts of existing books, and corporate imprints, can be created in large quantities for special needs. For more information, write to Special Markets/ Premium Sales, 1745 Broadway, MD 3-1, New York, New York 10019 or e-mail specialmarkets@ randomhouse.com.

PRINTED IN THE UNITED STATES OF AMERICA

10 9 8 7

Acknowledgments

Thanks to the Living Language team: Amanda D'Acierno, Dan Zitt, Suzanne McQuade, Erin Quirk, Heather Dalton, Fabrizio LaRocca, Siobhan O'Hare, Sophie Chin, Ann McBride, Tina Malaney, Sue Daulton, Alison Skrabek, Ciara Robinson, Tom Marshall. Special thanks to Sunhee Her and Emily Heo Moon.

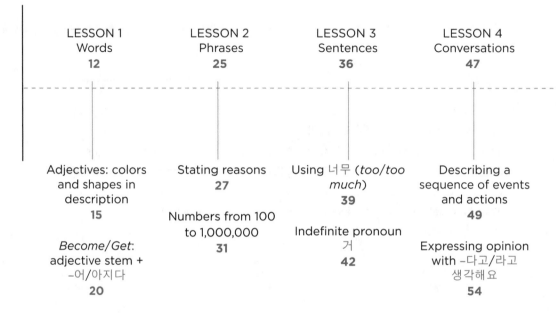
C O U R S E

OUTLINE

COURSE

UNIT 4: Talking about Health 174

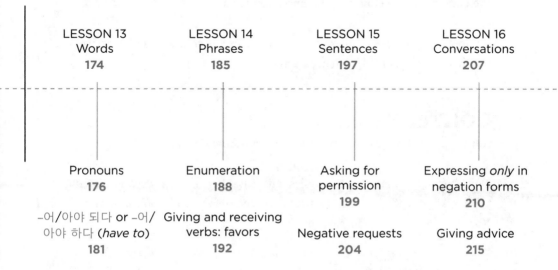
OUTLINE

How to Use This Course

Welcome to *Living Language Advanced Korean*!

Before we begin, let's go over what you'll see in this course. It's very easy to use, but this section will help you get started.

CONTENT

Advanced Korean is a continuation of *Intermediate Korean*.

Now that you've mastered the basics with *Essential* and *Intermediate Korean*, you'll take your Korean even further with a comprehensive look at more advanced Korean grammar and complex sentences.

UNITS

There are four units in this course. Each unit has four lessons arranged in a "building block" structure: the first lesson will present essential *words*, the second will introduce longer *phrases*, the third will teach *sentences*, and the fourth will show how everything works together in everyday *conversations*.

At the beginning of each unit is an introduction highlighting what you'll learn in that unit. At the end of each unit you'll find a self-graded Unit Quiz, which tests what you've learned.

LESSONS

There are four lessons per unit for a total of 16 lessons in the course. Each lesson has the following components:

- **Introduction** outlining what you will cover in the lesson.

- **Word Builder 1** (first lesson of the unit) presenting key words and phrases.

- **Phrase Builder 1** (second lesson of the unit) introducing longer phrases and expressions.

- **Sentence Builder 1** (third lesson of the unit) teaching sentences.

- **Conversation 1** (fourth lesson of the unit) for a natural dialogue that brings together important vocabulary and grammar from the unit.

- **Word/Phrase/Sentence/Conversation Practice 1** practicing what you learned in Word Builder 1, Phrase Builder 1, Sentence Builder 1, or Conversation 1.

- **Grammar Builder 1** guiding you through important Korean grammar that you need to know.

- **Work Out 1** for a comprehensive practice of what you saw in Grammar Builder 1.

- **Word Builder 2/Phrase Builder 2/Sentence Builder 2/Conversation 2** for more key words, phrases, or sentences, or a second dialogue.

- **Word/Phrase/Sentence/Conversation Practice 2** practicing what you learned in Word Builder 2, Phrase Builder 2, Sentence Builder 2, or Conversation 2.

- **Grammar Builder 2** for more information on Korean grammar.

- **Work Out 2** for a comprehensive practice of what you saw in Grammar Builder 2.

- **Drive It Home** ingraining an important point of Korean grammar for the long term.

- **Take It Furthers** providing extra information about the new vocabulary you just saw, expanding on certain grammar points, or introducing additional words and phrases.

- **Tips** or **Culture Notes** for helpful language tips or useful cultural information related to the lesson or unit.

- **Word Recall** reviewing important vocabulary and grammar from any of the previous lessons in *Advanced, Intermediate,* or *Essential Korean.*

- **How Did You Do?** outlining what you learned in the lesson.

UNIT QUIZ

At the end of each Unit, you'll see a **Unit Quiz.** The quizzes are self-graded so it's easy for you to test your progress and see if you should go back and review.

PROGRESS BAR

You will see a **Progress Bar** on each page that has course material. It indicates your current position within the unit and lets you know how much progress you're making. Each line in the bar represents a Grammar Builder section.

AUDIO

Look for the symbol ⊙ to help guide you through the audio as you're reading the book. It will tell you the name of the track to listen to for each section that has audio. When you see that symbol, start listening! If you don't see the symbol, then there isn't any audio for that section. The complete CD tracklisting is included on the accompanying CD, and can also be found on our website: **www. livinglanguage.com**.

The audio can be used on its own—in other words, without the book—when you're on the go. Whether in your car or at the gym, you can listen to the audio on its own to brush up on your pronunciation or review what you've learned in the book.

PRONUNCIATION GUIDE AND GRAMMAR SUMMARY

At the back of this book, you will find a **Pronunciation Guide** and **Grammar Summary**. The Pronunciation Guide provides information on Korean pronunciation. The Grammar Summary contains a brief overview of key Korean grammar you've learned.

GUIDE TO READING AND WRITING KOREAN

The Korean alphabet is a syllabic alphabet; you will learn how to read and write Korean gradually through this book and in the **Guide to Reading and Writing Korean** included with this course. Use the Guide to Reading and Writing Korean to practice reading and writing Korean in addition to using exercises in the coursebook.

FREE ONLINE TOOLS

Go to **www.livinglanguage.com/languagelab** to access your free online tools. The tools are organized around the lessons in this course, with audiovisual flashcards, as well as interactive games and quizzes for each lesson. These tools will help you to review and practice the vocabulary and grammar that you've seen in the lessons, providing some extra words and phrases related to the lesson's topic as well.

Unit 1:
Shopping

Welcome to your first unit of *Advanced Korean*! In Unit 1, you will learn some key expressions and vocabulary related to shopping for food and clothes. You will also learn how to use color words and numbers up to 1,000,000. By the end of the unit, you'll be able to talk about clothes and grocery shopping using key vocabulary. You'll be able to conjugate adjectives in the non-past tense, express *too* and *too much*, and state opinions with *I think that* .... You'll also be able to describe a sequence of events and actions and express reasoning. Ready to get started?

Lesson 1: Words

In this lesson you'll learn:

☐ how to use key vocabulary related to clothes and grocery shopping.

☐ adjectives for describing colors and shapes (ㅎ irregular).

☐ how to express *become/get* using –어/아지다.

Word Builder 1

⊙ 1A Word Builder 1

점원	*store clerk*
스웨터	*sweater*
셔츠	*shirt*

Using 너무 (*too/too much*)

Describing a sequence of events
and actions

Indefinite pronoun 거

Expressing opinion with
–다고/라고 생각해요

블라우스	*blouse*
바지	*pants*
청바지	*jeans*
치마	*skirt*
넥타이	*necktie*
모	*wool*
면	*cotton*
줄무늬	*stripes*
단색	*solid (color)*
디자인	*design*
사이즈	*size*
인기	*popularity*
계산	*payment*
현금	*cash*
신용카드	*credit card*
잔돈	*change*
천원	*1,000 won*
만원	*10,000 won*
환불하다	*to refund*
반환하다	*to return (goods)*
교환하다	*to exchange (goods)*
빨간	*red*
파란	*blue*
초록	*green*
노란	*yellow*
갈색	*brown*
회색	*gray*
분홍색	*pink*

Adjectives: colors and
shapes in description

Stating reasons

Become/Get: adjective
stem + –어/아지다

Numbers from 100 to 1,000,00

밝은	bright
어두운	dark
가벼운	light
무거운	heavy
짧은	short
긴	long
좀 큰	a little big (size of clothing)
넉넉한	comfortable
좁은	narrow
더운	hot
추운	cold
따뜻한	warm
시원한, 차가운	cool
생각하다	to think
찾다	to look for

✎ Word Practice 1

Translate the following words into Korean.

store clerk	1.
cotton	2.
stripes	3.
solid (color)	4.
popularity	5.
payment	6.
cash	7.
change	8.
to exchange	9.

Using 너무 (*too/too much*)

Describing a sequence of events
and actions

Indefinite pronoun 거

Expressing opinion with
–다고/라고 생각해요

dark	10.

ANSWER KEY
1. 점원 2. 면 3. 줄무늬 4. 단색 5. 인기 6. 계산 7. 현금 8. 잔돈 9. 교환하다 10. 어두운

Grammar Builder 1

▶ 1B Grammar Builder 1

ADJECTIVES: COLORS AND SHAPES IN DESCRIPTION

Let's look at the modification of various adjectives for color expressions. All
ㅎ adjectives drop ㅎ when they are used in front of the nouns, with a few
exceptions. One of these exceptions is *to be good*, 좋다.

INFINITIVES	ADJECTIVAL FORMS IN FRONT OF NOUNS: ㅎ MODIFICATION
하얗다 *to be white*	하얀
까맣다 *to be black*	까만
파랗다 *to be blue*	파란
노랗다 *to be yellow*	노란
빨갛다 *to be red*	빨간

좀 더 어두운 파란 색으로 없을까요?
Isn't there a little bit darker blue?

빨간 우산이 까만 우산보다 더 비싸요.
The red umbrella is more expensive than the black umbrella.

Stating reasons

Become/Get: adjective
stem + –어/아지다

Numbers from 100 to 1,000,000

Let's look at more modification of these adjectives using the different endings
we've learned. The ㅎ drops in front of vowels as seen in *Polite ending* –어/아요
variations and *Polite Past tense* –었/았어요 in the following chart. However, the
ㅎ does not drop in front of consonants, as seen in the examples of *Comment*
–네요 below.

INFINITIVES	POLITE ENDING –어/아요	POLITE PAST TENSE –었/았어요	COMMENT –네요
하얗다 *to be white*	하얘요	하얬어요	하얗네요
까맣다 *to be black*	까매요	까맸어요	까맣네요
파랗다 *to be blue*	파래요	파랬어요	파랗네요
노랗다 *to be yellow*	노래요	노랬어요	노랗네요
빨갛다 *to be red*	빨개요	빨갰어요	빨갛네요

✎ Work Out 1

A. Fill in the blank with the appropriate adjective based on the translation, then
change them into their appropriate form (if necessary) to complete the sentences.
Use polite forms.

1. 그 가방이 _____?

   Is that bag black?

   아니요, _____.

   No, it's red.

2. 이 영화가 _____?

   Is this movie long?

아니요, _____.

No, it's short.

3. 그 스웨터가 _____?

Is that sweater expensive?

아니요, _____.

No, it is cheap.

4. 치마를 새로 샀어요.

I bought a new skirt.

_____. (comment)

It is good. (comment)

5. 거실이 _____?

Is the living room bright?

아니요, ____지 않아요. 좀_____.

No, it isn't bright. It's a little dark.

B. Fill in the blank with the appropriate adjective from the list below, changing them into the appropriate form (if necessary), based on the translation. Use the polite form.

파랗다, 유명하다, 편리하다, 하얗다, 활발하다, 깨끗하다, 조용하다

1. 서울은 아주 _____도시예요.

Seoul is a very lively city.

2. 그 회사는 별로_____지 않아요.

That company is not so famous.

3. 제 아파트는 별로_____지 않아요.

   My apartment is not so clean.

4. 이 컴퓨터가 아주_____.

   This computer is very convenient.

5. 그 공원이 별로_____지 않아요.

   That park is not so quiet.

6. _____자켓은 여름에 시원해요.

   A white jacket is cool in summer.

7. _____바지가 더 잘 어울려요.

   The blue pants fit you better.

ANSWER KEY
A. 1. 까매요, 빨개요 2. 길어요, 짧아요 3. 비싸요, 싸요 4. 좋네요 5. 밝아요, 밝, 어두워요
B. 1. 활발한 2. 유명하 3. 깨끗하 4. 편리해요 5. 조용하 6. 하얀 7. 파란

Word Builder 2

▶ 1C Word Builder 2

주스	*juice*
청량음료	*soft drink*
상추	*lettuce*
양배추	*cabbage*
오이	*cucumber*
토마토	*tomato*
감자	*potato*
양파	*onion*
햄	*ham*

계란	egg
삶은 계란	boiled egg
빵	bread
치즈	cheese
버터	butter
피자	pizza
양념	seasoning
고추	chilli pepper
후추	black pepper
소금	salt
설탕	sugar
쇼핑카트	shopping cart
후라이드 치킨	fried chicken
가격	price
같은	same
전부	all
만약	if, in case
만들다	to make
부족하다	to be insufficient, to be short

✎ Word Practice 2

Translate the following words into Korean.

potato	1.
egg	2.
pepper	3.
salt	4.
sugar	5.

Adjectives: colors and
shapes in description

Stating reasons

Become/Get: adjective
stem + –어/아지다

Numbers from 100 to 1,000,000

bread	6.
price	7.
to be insufficient	8.
same	9.
all	10.

ANSWER KEY
1. 감자 2. 계란 3. 고추 4. 소금 5. 설탕 6. 빵 7. 가격 8. 부족하다 9. 같은 10. 전부

Grammar Builder 2

▶ 1D Grammar Builder 2

BECOME/GET: ADJECTIVE STEM + –어/아지다

You learned how to say *become a teacher* 선생님이 되다 and *become famous* 유명하게 되다 in *Intermediate Korean*. Now, let's learn how to say, for instance, *become expensive* and *become cold*. *Expensive* and *cold* are adjectives that denote conditional change; in Korean, we will use the –어/아 지다 form with these types of conditional adjectives. This expression refers to the change of measurable conditions such as price, weather, weight, height, etc.

비싸지다	*to become expensive*	싸지다	*to become inexpensive*
커지다	*to become big*	작아지다	*to become small (size)*
더워지다	*to become hot*	추워지다	*to become cold*
많아지다	*to become many/ much*	적어지다	*to become small (quantity)*
뜨거워지다	*to become hot (to the touch)*	차가워지다	*to become cool (to the touch)*
가벼워지다	*to become light*	무거워지다	*to become heavy*
높아지다	*to become high*	낮아지다	*to become low*

젊어지다	to become young (person)	낡아지다	to become old (goods)
밝아지다	to become bright	어두워지다	to become dark
재미있어지다	to become interesting	재미없어지다	to become uninteresting
따뜻해지다	to become warm	흐려지다	to become cloudy

These expressions can also be translated into English as *get*—*get expensive* and *get cold*—if it suits the context.

최근에 가격이 많이 비싸졌습니다.
Recently, prices became expensive.

7월이 되면 정말 더워집니다.
When July comes (lit: when it becomes July), it gets really hot.

10년 전에 산 제 청바지가 너무 낡아져서 새 것을 사야겠어요.
My jeans I bought ten years ago got old, so I should buy a new pair.

최근에 한국어를 배우고있는 학생들이 많아졌습니다.
The number of students who are learning Korean became many in recent days.

✎ Work Out 2

Translate the following Korean sentences into English.

1. 제 차가 낡아졌습니다.

_____

2. 방이 밝아졌습니다.

_____

3. 이 책이 재미있어졌습니다.

_____

4. 봄이 와서 따뜻해졌습니다.

_____

5. 11월이 되면 추워집니다.

_____

ANSWER KEY

1. *My car became/got old. 2. The room became/got bright. 3. This book became/got interesting. 4. Spring has come, so it became/got warm. 5. When November comes (lit: when it becomes November), it becomes/gets cold.*

✎ Drive It Home

Fill in the blanks with the appropriate words.

1. 이 영화는 _____.

This movie is not interesting.

2. 제 방은 ____지 않습니다.

My room is not bright.

3. 봄이 왔지만 _____지 않습니다.

Spring has come, but it's not warm.

4. 가방이 _____졌습니다.

The bag became light.

5. 정말 _____졌습니다.

It got very cold.

Using 너무 (*too/too much*)

Describing a sequence of events
and actions

Indefinite pronoun 거

Expressing opinion with
–다고/라고 생각해요

6. 커피 가격이 _____.

   The price of coffee became expensive.

7. 이 도시는 별로 _____지 않습니다.

   This town is not very famous.

8. 이 도서관은 별로_____지 않습니다.

   This library is not very quiet.

9. 12월인데 _____않네요.

   Even though it is December, it does not get cold.

ANSWER KEY
1. 재미없습니다 2. 밝 3. 따뜻하 4. 가벼워 5. 추워 6. 비싸졌습니다 7. 유명하 8. 조용하 9. 추워지지

🌐 Culture Note

The Korean unit of currency is the 원 (won). The exchange rate for the 원 has been roughly $1=1000 원 over the past ten years or so. With 1000 원, you can buy a snack or a soda in the grocery store. The Korean national bank (한국 은행 *hankuk eunhaeng*) issues money in both paper and coin form. The 1 원 and 5 원 coins are practically obsolete and out of use because their values are so low. The coins still in use are 10 원, 50 원, 100 원, and 500 원 coins. The paper money begins with 1,000 원, 5,000 원, 10,000 원, and 50,000 원 bills. The Korean government is planning to design a 100,000 원 bill, which will become the highest unit in paper money. Koreans do not use personal checks as Americans do. Instead, they use cash or money orders.

Adjectives: colors and
shapes in description

Stating reasons

Become/Get: adjective
stem + –어/아지다

Numbers from 100 to 1,000,000

How Did You Do?

Let's see how you did! By now, you should be able to:

☐ use key vocabulary related to clothes and grocery shopping. (Still unsure? Jump back to Word Builder 1 or Word Builder 2.)

☐ use adjectives to describe colors and shapes: ㅎ irregular. (Still unsure? Jump back to Grammar Builder 1.)

☐ express *become/get*: –어/아지다. (Still unsure? Jump back to Grammar Builder 2.)

✎ Word Recall

1. 리포트	a. *hair dye, hair color*
2. 5월	b. *right*
3. KTX	c. *report*
4. 바꾸다	d. *Korean bullet train*
5. 5층	e. *to keep someone waiting*
6. 염색	f. *to replace, to transfer (a phone line)*
7. 기다리게 하다	g. *May*
8. 길	h. *fifth floor*
9. 오른쪽	i. *street, road*
10. 소프트웨어	j. *software*

ANSWER KEY
1. c; 2. g; 3. d; 4. f; 5. h; 6. a; 7. e; 8. i; 9. b; 10. j

Lesson 2: Phrases

In this lesson you'll learn how to:

☐ state reasons with –(으)니까.

☐ count up to 1,000,000.

Phrase Builder 1

▶ 2A Phrase Builder 1

어서 오세요.	*Welcome (to our store).*
많이 기다리셨습니다.	*We have kept you waiting. (polite)*
어때요?	*How is it?*
정말	*really*
미디움으로요?	*Is medium okay?*
어떤 스웨터	*what kind of sweater*
백 퍼센트 모	*100% wool*
이 갈색 스웨터	*this brown sweater*
회색에 빨간 줄무늬가 있는 것/거	*the gray one with red stripes*
갈색이나 회색	*brown or gray*
좀 밝은 갈색	*a little brighter brown*
파란색이나 분홍색	*blue or pink*
예쁜색	*pretty color*
좀 작은	*a little small*
좀 짧은	*a little short*
단색인 것도	*the one in a solid color, too*
좋은 디자인	*good design*

인기가 많은	*very popular*
청바지와 바지에 다 어울려요.	*It goes with both jeans and pants.*
거스름돈 삼천 이백 원	*three thousand, two hundred won change*
얼마예요?	*How much is it?*
가격이 내렸어요.	*The price has been lowered.*
이걸로 주세요.	*Please give me this./I'll take this.*

✎ Phrase Practice 1

Translate the expressions below into Korean.

Welcome (to our store).	1.
How is it?	2.
really	3.
good design	4.
Is medium okay?	5.
100% wool	6.
brown or gray	7.
pretty color	8.
very popular	9.
How much is it?	10.

ANSWER KEY

1. 어서 오세요 2. 어때요? 3. 정말 4. 좋은 디자인 5. 미디움으로요? 6. 백 퍼센트 모 7. 갈색이나 회색 8. 예쁜 색 9. 인기가 많은 10. 얼마예요?

Grammar Builder 1

▶ 2B Grammar Builder 1

STATING REASONS

We learned earlier how to state a reason with the –어/아서 and –기 때문에 form. Just as in English with *for, because, so, since,* etc., there are other forms in Korean for stating reason. The third Korean form we will learn is –(으)니까. –(으)니까 acts like the English expression *so* or *therefore* in stating reason.

좀 작으니까 큰 사이즈로 교환해주세요.
It is a bit small, so please exchange this with a larger size.

이 스웨터가 가볍고 따뜻하니까 아주 좋네요.
This sweater is light and warm, so/therefore it is very good.

그 공원은 깨끗하고 조용하니까 이번 일요일에는 거기로 가요.
That park is clean and quiet, so let's go there this Sunday.

그 식당은 맛있고 별로 안 비싸니까 다음에 또 가고 싶어요.
That restaurant's food is delicious and not very expensive, so I want to go there again.

Let's look at the past tense variations with –(으)니까.

정미 씨가 A회사에서 인기가 많았으니까 B회사에서도 잘 할 거예요.
Ms. Jeong-Mi was popular in company A, so/therefore she will do well in company B.

지난 번에는 회색 스웨터를 샀으니까 이번에는 빨간색 스웨터를 사지요?
We bought a gray sweater last time, so this time how about buying a red sweater?

이번 주에 가격이 많이 내렸으니까 쇼핑을 하러 가야 겠네요.
The price went down a lot this week, so we should go shopping.

If you look carefully at the form variations, you'll see that the dummy vowel
으 appears after the past tense form 었/았 since the past forms end with a
consonant. Use 으니까 after words ending in a consonant and 니까 after words
ending in a vowel.

Note that you can state three or more reasons using the same structure. It can also
be used to give just one reason.

오늘은 비가 오고, 춥고, 게다가 바람도 세니까 나가고 싶지 않아요.
*Today it's raining, cold, and furthermore, the wind is strong, so I don't want to go
out.*

눈이 오니까 집에 있죠.
It's snowing, so let's stay at home.

✎ Work Out 1

Fill in the blanks with the appropriate words to complete the sentences.

1. 제 차가 낡고 작_____새 차를 사고 싶어요.

   My car is old and small, so I want to buy a new car.

2. 눈이 오_____집에 있죠.

   It is snowing so let's stay at home.

3. 이 스웨터가 크고 비싸_____안 살 거예요.

   This sweater is large and expensive, so I won't buy it.

Using 너무 (*too/too much*)

Describing a sequence of events
and actions

Indefinite pronoun 거

Expressing opinion with
–다고/라고 생각해요

4. 오늘은 따뜻하_____좋네요.

Today is warm, so it's good.

5. 이 책이 길고 재미없_____안 읽을 거예요.

This book is long and boring, so I won't read it.

ANSWER KEY
1. 으니까 2. 니까 3. 니까 4. 니까 5. 으니까

Phrase Builder 2

▶ 2C Phrase Builder 2

오늘 파티	today's party
얼마나 많은 사람들	how many people
맥주 세 상자	three boxes of beer
와인 여섯 병	six bottles of wine
백포도주와 적포도주 각 세 병 씩	white wine and red wine, three bottles each
한국 거 열 병	ten bottles of the Korean one
미국 거 열 병	ten bottles of the American one
한국 거와 미국 거	a Korean one and an American one
한 병에 오천 원	five thousand won for one bottle
같은 가격	the same price
같은 가격의 적포도주	red wine of the same price
좀 너무 비싼데요.	It's a little too expensive.
좀 싼 거	a slightly cheaper one
(−을/를) 샐러드에 (−을/를) 넣다	put into a salad
다 얼마예요?	how much all together
집을 떠나다	leave home
맞습니다.	That's right.

Adjectives: colors and
shapes in description

Stating reasons

Become/Get: adjective
stem + –어/아지다

Numbers from 100 to 1,000,000

✏ Phrase Practice 2

Fill in the missing words below.

1. 얼마나 많은_____

   how many people

2. 맥주 세_____

   three boxes of beer

3. 백포도주와 적포도주 각 세 병_____

   white wine and red wine, three bottles each

4. 한국 거와 미국_____

   a Korean one and an American one

5. 같은_____

   same price

6. 좀_____거

   a little cheaper one

7. _____얼마예요

   how much all together

8. 집을_____

   leave home

ANSWER KEY

1. 사람들 2. 상자 3. 씩 4. 거 5. 가격 6. 싼 7. 다 8. 떠나다

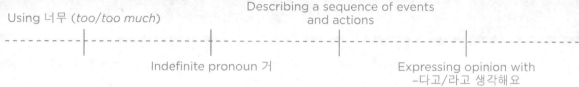
Grammar Builder 2

▷ 2D Grammar Builder 2

NUMBERS FROM 100 TO 1,000,000

You have already learned how to count to 100. Now, let's learn how to count to 1,000,000. First, let's learn how to count from 100 to 999.

백	100
이백	200
삼백	300
사백	400
오백	500
육백	600
칠백	700
팔백	800
구백	900

If you want to say *158*, you just need to combine 백, 오십, and 팔 to get 백 오십 팔.

이백 육십 삼	263
삼백 십 이	312
사백 팔	408
오백 칠십 구	579
육백 삼십 삼	633
칠백 구십 일	791
팔백 삼십 오	835
구백 구십 구	999

Next, let's learn how to count from 1000 to 9000.

천	1000

Adjectives: colors and
shapes in description

Stating reasons

Become/Get: adjective
stem + –어/아지다

Numbers from 100 to 1,000,00

이천	2000
삼천	3000
사천	4000
오천	5000
육천	6000
칠천	7000
팔천	8000
구천	9000

If you want to say *1600*, combine 천 and 육백 to get 천 육백. If you want to say *1652*, combine 천, 육백, 오십, 이 to get 천 육백 오십 이.

이천 삼백 십	2310
삼천 팔백 칠십 오	3875
사천 구백 육십 육	4966
오천 이백 사십 오	5245
육천 팔백 일	6801
칠천 사백 삼십 이	7432
팔천 구백 십 육	8916
구천 구백 구십 구	9999

Now, let's learn how to count from 10,000 to 1,000,000.

만	10,000
이만	20,000
삼만	30,000
사만	40,000
오만	50,000
육만	60,000
칠만	70,000

Using 너무 (*too/too much*)

Describing a sequence of events
and actions

Indefinite pronoun 거

Expressing opinion with
–다고/라고 생각해요

팔만	80,000
구만	90,000
십만	100,000
이십만	200,000
삼십만	300,000
사십만	400,000
오십만	500,000
육십만	600,000
칠십만	700,000
팔십만	800,000
구십만	900,000
백만	1,000,000

To say *56,700*, combine 오만, 육천, 칠백 to get 오만 육천 칠백. Likewise, to say *716,892*, combine each unit to get 칠십 일만 육천 팔백 구십 이.

육십만 천 삼백 이십 일	601,321
칠십 일만 오천 사백 삼십	715,430
구십 구만 구천 구백 구십 구	999,999

✎ Work Out 2

Write the following numbers in Korean.

1. *303* _____

2. *685* _____

3. *899* _____

4. *971* _____

5. *1,320* _____

Adjectives: colors and
shapes in description

Stating reasons

Become/Get: adjective
stem + –어/아지다

Numbers from 100 to 1,000,000

6. *2,007* _____

7. *3,866* _____

8. *8,682* _____

9. *11,100* _____

10. *24,318* _____

11. *83,688* _____

12. *90,877* _____

13. *101,134* _____

14. *265,359* _____

ANSWER KEY
1. 삼백 삼 2. 육백 팔십 오 3. 팔백 구십 구 4. 구백 칠십 일 5. 천 삼백 이십 6. 이천 칠 7. 삼천 팔백
육십 육 8. 팔천 육백 팔십 이 9. 만 천 백 10. 이만 사천 삼백 십팔 11. 팔만 삼천 육백 팔십 팔 12. 구만
팔백 칠십 칠 13. 십만 천 백 삼십 사 14. 이십 육만 오천 삼백 오십 구

✎ Drive It Home

Fill in the blanks with the appropriate words.

1. 이 스웨터가 가볍_____따뜻하_____아주 좋네요.

   This sweater is light and warm, and so very nice.

2. 좀 작_____큰 사이즈_____교환해주세요.

   It is a bit small so please exchange this with a larger size.

3. 그 공원은 깨끗하_____조용하_____이번 일요일에는 거기로 가요.

   That park is clean and quiet so let's go there this Sunday.

4. 지난 번에는 회색 스웨터를 샀_____이번에는 빨간색 스웨터_____사지요?

   We bought a gray sweater last time so this time how about buying a red sweater?

5. 이번 주에 가격이 많이 내렸_____쇼핑을 하러 가야____네요.

The price went down a lot this week, so we should go shopping.

6. 이____

200

7. 삼____

300

8. 사____

4,000

9. 오____

5,000

10. 육____

60,000

ANSWER KEY

1. 고, 니까 2. 으니까, 로 3. 고, 니까 4. 으니까, 를 5. 으니까, 겠 6. 백 7. 백 8. 천 9. 천 10. 만

☀ Tip!

Check out the advertisements for automobiles, furniture stores, department stores, supermarkets, electric appliance stores, etc., in the newspaper, magazines, or on the Web, and try saying the prices out loud in Korean. Also, you can check the advertisements by real estate companies, and try giving the prices of houses in Korean. In this way, you can practice using a wide range of numbers.

How Did You Do?

Let's see how you did! By now, you should be able to:

☐ state reasons using –(으)니까. (Still unsure? Jump back to Grammar Builder 1.)

Adjectives: colors and
shapes in description

Stating reasons

Become/Get: adjective
stem + –어/아지다

Numbers from 100 to 1,000,000

☐ count up to 1,000,000. (Still unsure? Jump back to Grammar Builder 2.)

✎ Word Recall

1. 소파	a. *bed*
2. 침대	b. *sofa*
3. 보이다	c. *to run*
4. 돌다	d. *to walk*
5. 걷다	e. *to be able to be seen, to be visible*
6. 뛰다	f. *to cross*
7. 왼쪽	g. *to turn*
8. 되다	h. *high-rise building*
9. 건너다	i. *to become*
10. 고층 빌딩	j. *left*

ANSWER KEY
1. b; 2. a; 3. e; 4. g; 5. d; 6. c; 7. j; 8. i; 9. f; 10. h

Lesson 3: Sentences

In this lesson you'll learn how to:

☐ express *too* and *too much*.

☐ use the indefinite pronoun *one*.

Sentence Builder 1

▷ 3A Sentence Builder 1

스웨터는 어디에 있어요?	*Where are the sweaters? (polite)*

넥타이는 저기에 있어요.	*The neckties are there. (polite)*
어떤 스웨터를 찾으세요?	*What kind of sweater are you looking for? (polite)*
갈색이나 회색으로 100퍼센트 모 스웨터가 있어요?	*Do you have one made of 100% wool and either brown or gray?*
이 갈색 스웨터는 어떠세요?	*What about this brown sweater? (polite)*
더 밝은 갈색이 좋겠는데요...	*I prefer a little brighter brown ...*
저 회색에 빨간색 줄무늬디자인이 좋은 것 같은데요.	*That gray one with red stripes has a nice design.*
이 스웨터가 인기가 많습니다.	*This sweater is popular.*
가볍고 따뜻해서 좋아요.	*It's light and warm, so it's good.*
좀 짧지 않아요?	*Isn't it a little bit short?*
좀 짧은 것 같네요.	*It may be a little short.*
청바지하고 바지에 다 어울려요.	*It goes with both jeans and pants.*
치마하고 어울리는 것 같아요.	*I think it goes with a skirt.*
이걸로 단색이 있어요?	*Do you have one in a solid color?*
파란색이나 분홍색이라면 있습니다.	*If it's blue or pink, we have it. (polite)*
파란색이 예쁘네요.	*The blue one is pretty.*
이건 16,800원입니다.	*This one is 16,800 won.*
2만 원이었는데 세일이라서 가격이 내렸어요.	*It was 20,000 won, but has been priced down because it's on sale.*
사이즈는 미디움이 좋으세요?	*Is medium size okay?*
5만 원이 있어요.	*I have 50,000 won.*
현금으로 하세요?	*Are you paying cash? (lit: As for payment, is it by cash?)*
카드로 해 주세요.	*With a card, please.*
이만 원 받았습니다.	*I received 20,000 won.*

Adjectives: colors and
shapes in description

Stating reasons

Become/Get: adjective
stem + –어/아지다

Numbers from 100 to 1,000,000

| 거스름돈 3,200원입니다. | It's 3,200 won change. |

✎ Sentence Practice 1

Fill in the missing words in each of the following sentences.

1. 스웨터는 어디_____있어요?

   Where are the sweaters? (polite)

2. 어떤 스웨터_____찾으세요?

   What kind of sweater are you looking for? (polite)

3. 이 갈색 스웨터_____어떠세요?

   What about this brown sweater?

4. 이 스웨터가 인기_____많습니다.

   This sweater is popular.

5. 가볍고_____좋아요.

   It's light and warm, so it's good.

6. 청바지하고 바지_____다 어울려요.

   It goes with both jeans and pants.

7. 치마_____어울리는 것 같아요.

   I think it goes with a skirt.

8. 이걸_____단색이 있어요?

   Do you have one in a solid color?

   ANSWER KEY
   1. 에 2. 를 3. 는 4. 가 5. 따뜻해서 6. 에 7. 하고/에 8. 로

Grammar Builder 1

▶ 3B Grammar Builder 1

USING 너무 (*TOO/TOO MUCH*)

너무 (*too/too much*) is used frequently in Korean conversation. It is used to emphasize a point, just as *really* might be used in English. Let's see some examples.

너무 작아요.
It's too small.

너무 커요.
It's too big.

너무 좋아요!
It's too good!

이 책은 너무 어려워요.
This book is too difficult.

지금 아파트는 너무 불편해서 새 아파트를 찾고 있어요.
The current apartment is too inconvenient, so I am looking for a new apartment.

일요일에 12시까지 잤어요. 좀 너무 많이 잤어요.
I slept until noon on Sunday. I slept a little too much.

어제 맥주를 너무 많이 마셔서 오늘은 술을 안 마실 거예요.
I drank too much beer yesterday, so I won't drink alcohol today.

Adjectives: colors and
shapes in description

Stating reasons

Become/Get: adjective
stem + –어/아지다

Numbers from 100 to 1,000,000

✎ Work Out 1

Complete the sentences using the expression 너무.

1. 오늘 숙제는_____쉽네요.

   Today's homework is too easy.

2. 이 잡지는 너무_____.

   This magazine is too boring.

3. 이 공원은 너무_____.

   This park is too quiet.

4. 어제 와인을 너무 많이_____.

   I drank too much wine yesterday.

5. 오늘 너무 많이_____.

   I ate too much today.

6. 월요일에 너무 공부를 많이_____.

   I studied too much on Monday.

7. _____많이 샀어요.

   I bought too much.

ANSWER KEY
1. 너무 2. 재미없네요 3. 조용하네요 4. 마셨어요 5. 먹었어요 6. 했어요 7. 너무

Sentence Builder 2

▶ 3C Sentence Builder 2

오늘 파티에 몇 명이나 와요?	*How many people are coming to the party today?*

Using 너무 (*too/too much*)

Describing a sequence of events
and actions

Indefinite pronoun 거

Expressing opinion with
–다고/라고 생각해요

저는 열 명 쯤 생각하고 있는데요.	*About ten people, I think.*
맥주 30병 쯤 사면 되겠네요?	*It will be okay if we buy about thirty bottles of beer, right?*
한국 맥주 20병을 사는 것이 어때요?	*How about buying twenty bottles of Korean beer?*
좋은 생각이네요.	*That's a good idea.*
한 병에 삼만 원이나 하네요.	*It is as much as 30,000 won per bottle.*
그건 좀 너무 비싼데요.	*It's a little too expensive.*
그럼 이건 어때요?	*Then how about this one?*
그건 한 병에 오천 원이에요.	*That's 5,000 won for a bottle.*
같은 가격으로 적포도주도 있어요.	*There is also red wine at the same price.*
카트에 저 백포도주 세 병하고 이 적포도주 세 병을 넣을게요.	*I will put those three bottles of white wine and these three bottles of red wine in the cart.*
삶은 계란을 만들어서 샐러드에 넣으면 좋겠네요.	*It will be good if we make boiled eggs and put them in the salad.*
초밥하고 피자를 살 건데 다 얼마나 할까요?	*Since we will buy sushi and pizza, about how much will it be all together?*
충분하지 않으면, 신용 카드를 쓸거니까 괜찮을 거예요.	*If it's not enough, I will use a credit card, so it will be okay.*

✎ Sentence Practice 2

Fill in the missing words in each of the following sentences.

1. 저는 열 명 쯤 생각하고 있_____.

   About ten people, I think.

2. 맥주 30병_____사면 되겠네요?

   It will be okay if we buy about thirty bottles of beer, right?

Adjectives: colors and
shapes in description

Stating reasons

Become/Get: adjective
stem + –어/아지다

Numbers from 100 to 1,000,00

3. 한국 맥주 20병을 사는 것이_____?

   How about buying twenty bottles of Korean beer?

4. 좋은_____이네요.

   That's a good idea.

5. 그건 한 병_____5,000원이에요.

   That's 5,000 won for a bottle.

6. 그건 좀_____비싼데요.

   It's a little too expensive.

7. 초밥하고_____살 건데 다 얼마나 할까요?

   Since we will buy sushi and pizza, how much will it be all together?

8. 충분하지 않으면, 신용 카드를_____거니까 괜찮을 거예요.

   If it's not enough, I will use a credit card, so it will be okay.

ANSWER KEY
1. 는데요 2. 쯤 3. 어때요 4. 생각 5. 에 6. 너무 7. 피자를 8. 쓸

Grammar Builder 2

▷ 3D Grammar Builder 2

INDEFINITE PRONOUN 거

The indefinite pronoun 거 usually corresponds to English *one* or *a thing* and replaces a noun which has already been introduced. Note how this occurs in English:

This red shirt is nice. But I don't like that blue one.

This sweater is short. Do you have a long one?

Now let's look at how this occurs in Korean sentences with 거.

이 붉은 색 셔츠가 좋네요. 그런데 그 파란 거는 싫어요.
This red shirt is nice. But I don't like that blue one.

이 스웨터는 짧아요. 긴 거 있어요?
This sweater is short. Do you have a long one?

The indefinite pronoun 거, like the English *one*, is always accompanied by modifiers, such as an adjective or a demonstrative, or a combination of the two. Also, a possessor word can appear before 거. Finally, note that in shortened expressions, 거 + 를 (object marker) is often abbreviated to 걸; likewise, 거 + 는 (topic marker) becomes 건 and 거 + 이 (subject marker) becomes 게. (These are contractions comparable to English *do* + *not* into *don't*.)

가볍고 따뜻한 거를 주세요. → 가볍고 따뜻한 걸 주세요.
Please give me a light and warm one.

저 파란 거는 청바지예요. → 저 파란 건 청바지예요.
The blue ones are blue jeans.

You'll also see 거 omitted in possessives. In this case, it is mandatory that you omit the possessive particle 의.

스미스 씨의 차는 새 거지만 이 씨 거는 오래됐네요.
Mr. Smith's car is a new one, but Mr. Lee's is old.

제 가방은 무거운데 제 여동생 거는 가벼워요.
My bag is heavy, but my younger sister's is light.

As you can see in the last two examples above, when they appear next to each other in a sentence (as in 이 씨 거는 *but Mr. Lee's* and 제 여동생 거는 *my*

Adjectives: colors and
shapes in description

Stating reasons

Become/Get: adjective
stem + –어/아지다

Numbers from 100 to 1,000,00(

younger sister's) 의 after 여동생 is omitted. Non-omitted forms would have been 이 씨의 거는 and 제 여동생의 거는 respectively, but these non-omitted forms are not used in everyday conversation, so always try to use the omitted forms.

✎ Work Out 2

Translate the following Korean sentences into English.

1. 회색에 빨간색 줄무늬가 있는 거로 주세요.

   _____

2. 지난 번에는 회색 셔츠를 샀으니까 이번에는 빨간 거로 주세요.

   _____

3. 인기가 많은 건 뭐예요?

   _____

4. 예쁜 거로 주세요.

   _____

5. 큰 거로 살 거예요.

   _____

ANSWER KEY

1. *Give me the gray one with red stripes.* 2. *Last time I bought a gray shirt, so this time, please give me one in red color.* 3. *What is the popular one?* 4. *Please give me a pretty one.* 5. *I will buy a big one.*

✎ Drive It Home

Fill in the blanks with the appropriate words to complete the sentences. Use the polite form.

1. 서울의 커피숍은_____비싸요.

   Coffee shops in Seoul are too expensive.

2. 이 책은 너무_____.

   This book is too difficult.

3. 이 블라우스는 좀 너무_____?

   This blouse is a little too big, isn't it?

4. 지금 아파트는 너무_____.

   The current apartment is too inconvenient.

5. 어제 맥주를 너무_____ 마셨어요.

   I drank too much beer yesterday.

6. 이 빨간 셔츠가 좋아요. 하지만 저 파란_____는 싫어요.

   I like this red shirt. But I don't like that blue one.

7. 이 스웨터는 짧아요. 긴_____있어요?

   This sweater is short. Do you have a long one?

8. 스미스 씨의 차는 새 건데 이 씨_____는 오래됐어요.

   Mr. Smith's car is new, but Mr. Lee's is old.

9. 제 가방은 무거운데 제 여동생_____는 가벼워요.

   My bag is heavy, but my younger sister's is light.

Adjectives: colors and
shapes in description

Stating reasons

Become/Get: adjective
stem + –어/아지다

Numbers from 100 to 1,000,00

ANSWER KEY

1. 너무 2. 어려워요 3. 크지요 4. 불편해요 5. 많이 6. 거 7. 거 8. 거 9. 거

Tip!

Look around your bedroom, living room, kitchen, yard, or another area of your
house, and describe the objects you see using adjectives you've learned so far. For
instance, you can describe a sofa, table, bookshelf, refrigerator, flowers, and so on.
Of course, you can also do this task at your workplace or school for more practice.

How Did You Do?

Let's see how you did! By now, you should be able to:

☐ express *too* and *too much*. (Still unsure? Jump back to Grammar Builder 1.)

☐ use the indefinite pronoun *one*. (Still unsure? Jump back to Grammar Builder 2.)

✎ Word Recall

1. 영어   a. *Chinese (person)*

2. 영국사람   b. *Spanish (language)*

3. 중국사람   c. *German (person)*

4. 독일사람   d. *English (language)*

5. 프랑스사람   e. *English (person)*

6. 프랑스어   f. *French (language)*

7. 멕시코사람   g. *French (person)*

8. 스페인사람   h. *Canadian (person)*

9. 캐나다사람   i. *Mexican (person)*

10. 스페인어   j. *Spanish (person)*

ANSWER KEY

1. d; 2. e; 3. a; 4. c; 5. g; 6. f; 7. i; 8. j; 9. h; 10. b

Using 너무 (*too/too much*)

Describing a sequence of events
and actions

Indefinite pronoun 거

Expressing opinion with
–다고/라고 생각해요

Lesson 4: Conversations

In this lesson you'll learn how to:

☐ describe a sequence of events and actions.

☐ state opinions with *I think that*.

🎧 Conversation 1

▶ 4A Conversation 1

Ms. Mansoo came to the women's section of a department store in Seoul to buy a sweater.

점원: 어서 오세요!

만수: 스웨터는 어디에 있어요?

점원: 스웨터는 저기에 있는데요, 어떤 스웨터를 찾으세요?

만수: 100퍼센트 모로 된 거로 갈색이나 회색 있어요?

점원: 그럼 이 갈색은 어떠세요?

만수: 좀 밝은 갈색이 좋겠는데요. 아, 저 회색에 빨간 줄무늬가 있는 거가 디자인이 좋네요.

점원: 이거요? 네, 이 스웨터가 아주 인기가 많습니다. 가볍고 아주 따뜻해서 좋아요.

만수: 좀 짧지 않아요?

점원: 좀 짧을 수 있지만 청바지하고 바지에 둘 다 잘 어울려요.

만수: 단색으로도 있어요?

점원: 파란색이나 분홍색이라면 있습니다. 이게 파란색이고 이게 분홍색이에요.

만수: 파란색이 예쁘네요. 얼마예요?

점원: 이건 16,800원이에요. 20,000원이었는데 세일이라서 가격이 내렸습니다.

만수: 그럼 이걸로 주세요.

Salesperson:	*Welcome!*
Mansoo:	*Where are the sweaters?*
Salesperson:	*The sweaters are there, but what kind of sweater are you looking for?*
Mansoo:	*Do you have one that's made of 100% wool, and brown or gray?*
Salesperson:	*Then, what about this brown?*
Mansoo:	*I would like a little brighter brown. Oh, that gray one with red stripes has a nice design.*
Salesperson:	*This one? This sweater is very popular. It's light and very warm, so it's good.*
Mansoo:	*Isn't it a little bit short?*
Salesperson:	*It can be a little short, but I think it will go well with both jeans and a pair of pants.*
Mansoo:	*Do you also have one in a solid color?*
Salesperson:	*If it's blue or pink, we have it. This is blue, and this is pink.*
Mansoo:	*The blue is pretty. How much is this?*
Salesperson:	*This one is 16,800 won. It was 20,000 won, but has been priced down because it's on sale.*
Mansoo:	*I'll take this one then.*

Take It Further 1

When you enter stores and restaurants, salespeople, waitresses or waiters will say 어서 오세요 (*welcome*) or even more formally, 어서 오십시오 to you almost every time. When the main business in these shops or restaurants is over, the typical parting term would be 안녕히 가세요 on the clerk's side, and you would most likely say 안녕히 계세요 to them as you leave. Some salespeople may say 또 오세요 (*Please come again*) which is another common term for saying good-bye on the clerk's side.

Using 너무 (*too/too much*)

Describing a sequence of events
and actions

Indefinite pronoun 거

Expressing opinion with
–다고/라고 생각해요

✎ Conversation Practice 1

Fill in the blanks in the following sentences with the missing words. If you're
unsure of the answer, listen to the conversation one more time.

1. 스웨터는 저기에 있는데요,_____스웨터를 찾으세요?

2. 이거요? 네, 이 스웨터가 아주_____많습니다.

3. 좀 짧을 수 있지만 청바지하고 바지____둘 다 잘 어울려요.

4. 단색_____도 있어요?

5. 그럼 이걸_____주세요.

ANSWER KEY
1. 어떤 2. 인기가 3. 에 4. 으로 5. 로

Grammar Builder 1
▶ 4B Grammar Builder 1

DESCRIBING A SEQUENCE OF EVENTS AND ACTIONS

The sentence connector –어 /아서 form was introduced in *Intermediate Korean*,
where you learned and practiced this in present and past tenses. The –어 /아서
form of verbs is used for two main functions depending on the situation:

1. to describe a sequence of events and actions, and

2. to explain a reason.

Remember the first action/event phrase containing –어 /아서 does not mark
the past tense; the past tense is marked only in the main verb at the end of the
sentence.

Adjectives: colors and
shapes in description

Stating reasons

Become/Get: adjective
stem + –어/아지다

Numbers from 100 to 1,000,00

슈퍼마켓에 가서 상추와 오이를 샀어요.

I went to a supermarket and bought lettuce and cucumbers.

한국에 가서 한국어를 일년 동안 배웠어요.

I went to Korea and studied Korean for a year.

You can theoretically connect any number of events or actions using the –어/
아서 form of verbs, but very long sequences would be difficult to process, and
are usually divided up into two or more sentences. For instance, if you want
to describe your daily routine, you would need several sentences to list all the
activities you engage in every day.

아침 7시에 일어나서 샤워를 하고 아침을 먹고 신문을 읽고 여덟 시에 집을
나가서 회사에 가요. 12시까지 일을 하고 점심을 먹고서 1시에는 미팅에
참석해요. 그 후에 리포트를 쓰고 회사에서 6시에 나가서 집에 7시에
도착해요. 저녁을 먹고, 텔레비전을 보고 목욕을 하고서 열한 시 반에 잠을
자요.

*I wake up at seven in the morning, take a shower, eat breakfast, read a newspaper,
leave home at eight, and go to work (lit: the company). I work until twelve, eat lunch
and attend a meeting at one. After that, I write a report, leave the company at six,
and arrive home at seven. I eat dinner, watch TV, take a bath, and go to sleep at
eleven thirty.*

Note that the enumeration is done with another sentence connector –고 *and*. The
–어/아서 form at times appears after 고 as a combined form: –고서, which has
the meaning of *after that*, indicating the finishing of one event followed by the
start of another.

Indefinite pronoun 거   Expressing opinion with
                                              –다고/라고 생각해요

✎ Work Out 1

Fill in the blanks below with the appropriate –어 /아서 or –고서 form of the
verbs in parentheses. Pay close attention to the English translation to determine
whether you will use –어 /아서 or –고서 .

1. 선생님께_____여기로 왔어요. (말씀드리다)

   I talked with a teacher and then came here.

2. 와인 두 병을_____파티에 갔어요. (사다)

   I bought two bottles of wine and then went to a party.

3. 잡지를 읽고 음악을_____잠을 잤어요. (듣다)

   I read a magazine, listened to the music, and went to bed.

4. 부산에서 친구를_____영화를 보고 식당에 가서 저녁을 먹었어요. (만나다)

   I met my friend in Busan, saw a movie, and went to a restaurant, and had dinner.

5. 대학을 졸업하고 한국에서 유학하고 한국어를 이 년 동안_____영어를
   가르쳤어요. (배우다)

   I graduated from a university, studied abroad in Japan, studied Japanese for two

   years, and after that taught English.

   ANSWER KEY
   1. 말씀드리고서 2. 사서 3. 듣고서 4. 만나서 5. 배우고서

▣ Conversation 2

▶ 4C Conversation 2

Mr. Collins is at a supermarket with his friend Ms. Jin-Hee in order to get some
food and beverages for their party.

콜린스: 오늘 파티에 몇 명이나 와요?

Adjectives: colors and
shapes in description

Stating reasons

Become/Get: adjective
stem + –어/아지다

Numbers from 100 to 1,000,00(

진희: 열 명쯤 생각하고 있는데요.

콜린스: 그럼 맥주 삼십 병하고 와인 여섯 병 쯤 사면 되겠네요?

진희: 네. 맥주는 한국 맥주로 스무 병하고 미국 맥주로 열 병 사면
          어때요?

콜린스: 좋은 생각이네요. 그리고 와인은 백포도주 세 병과 적포도주 세
          병을 사면 좋겠지요?

진희: 네, 그럼 이 백포도주는 어때요?

콜린스: 한 병에 삼만 원이나 하네요. 그건 좀 너무 비싼데요. 좀 더 싼
          거 있어요?

진희: 그럼 이건 어때요? 한 병에 이만 오천 원이네요. 같은 가격으로
          적포도주도 있어요.

콜린스: 네, 그럼 카트에 저 백포도주 세 병하고 이 적포도주 세 병을
          넣을게요.

진희: 그리고 상추, 오이, 토마토, 햄을 사서 샐러드를 만드는 거
          어때요?

콜린스: 좋아요. 그럼 계란도 사서 삶은 계란을 만들어서 샐러드에
          넣으면 좋겠네요.

진희: 네, 그럼 초밥하고 피자도 살 거니까 전부 얼마지요?

콜린스: 저는 9만 원 쯤 있어요.

진희: 저는 12만 원쯤 있어요. 현금이 부족하면 신용카드를 쓰면
          되니까 괜찮아요.

콜린스: 그렇군요.

Collins: *How many people are coming to today's party?*

Jin-Hee: *I think about ten people.*

Collins: *Then, it will be good if we buy thirty bottles of beer and about six
           bottles of wine, right?*

Jin-Hee: *Yes. As for beer, what about buying twenty bottles of Korean beer
           and ten bottles of American beer?*

Collins: *That's a good idea. And as for wine, it will be good if we buy three
           bottles of white wine and three bottles of red wine, right?*

Jin-Hee: *Yes. Then, what about this white wine?*

Using 너무 (*too/too much*)

Describing a sequence of events
and actions

Indefinite pronoun 거

Expressing opinion with
–다고/라고 생각해요

Collins:	That's thirty thousand won for a bottle. That's a little too expensive. Isn't there a cheaper one?
Jin-Hee:	Then, what about this one? It's twenty five thousand won for one bottle. There is also red wine at the same price.
Collins:	Okay. Then, I will put three bottles each of that white wine and this red wine into the cart.
Jin-Hee:	And, what about buying lettuce, cucumbers, tomatoes, and ham, and making a salad?
Collins:	Okay. Then, it will be good if we also buy eggs, make boiled eggs, and put them in the salad.
Jin-Hee:	And then, since we will buy sushi and pizza, how much will it be all together?
Collins:	I have about 90,000 won.
Jin-Hee:	As for me, I have about 120,000 won. If we are short on cash, I will use a credit card, so it's okay.
Collins:	Sounds good. (lit: Oh that is so.)

✎ Conversation Practice 2

Fill in the blanks in the following sentences with the missing words. If you're
unsure of the answer, listen to the conversation one more time.

1. 열 명쯤_____있는데요.

2. 그럼 맥주 삼십 병하고 와인 여섯 병 쯤_____되겠네요?

3. 그건 좀 너무 비싼데요. 좀_____싼 거 있어요?

4. 그리고 상추, 오이, 토마토, 햄을 사서 샐러드를_____거 어때요?

5. 현금이 부족하면 신용카드를 쓰면_____괜찮아요.

ANSWER KEY
1. 생각하고 2. 사면 3. 더 4. 만드는 5. 되니까

Grammar Builder 2

▶ 4D Grammar Builder 2

EXPRESSING OPINION WITH –다고/라고 생각해요

If you want to express your opinion by saying *I think (that)* ... you will use the
following grammar patterns:

Present form of verbs/adjectives (–ㄴ/는) + 다고 생각하다
Present form of copula 이다/아니다 + 라고 생각하다
Future tense ㄹ/을 거 + 라고 생각하다
Past form of verbs –ㅆ/었/았 + 다고 생각하다

A: 이 후라이드 치킨은 어때요?
How's this fried chicken?
B: 정말 맛있다고 생각해요.
I think it's very delicious.

A: 오늘 민아 씨가 바쁘다고 생각하세요?
Do you think Ms. Min-Ah is busy today?
B: 아니요, 오늘은 안 바쁜데요 ...
No, I think she is not busy, but ...

A: 정민 씨는 대학생이에요?
Is Ms. Jeong-Min a college student?
B: 아니요, 대학생이 아니라고 생각해요. 작년에 회사에서 일하고 있었어요.
No, I think she is not a college student. She was working at a company last year.

A: 콜린스 씨가 오늘 사무실에 올 거라고 생각하세요?
Do you think Mr. Collins will come to the office today?
B: 네, 올 거예요.
Yes, I think he will come.

A: 어제 진수 씨가 미팅에 참석했어요?

Did Mr. Jin-Soo attend the meeting yesterday?

B: 네, 참석했다고 생각하는데요 . . .

Yes, I think he attended.

The following are more examples of statements with –라/다고 생각합니다.

로페즈 씨는 중국사람이 아니라고 생각합니다.

I think Ms. Lopez is not Chinese.

스웨터가 별로 안 싸다고 생각합니다.

I think this sweater is not that cheap.

✎ Work Out 2

Translate the following Korean sentences into English.

1. 이 선생님 부부가 중국사람이라고 생각하세요?

   _____

2. 이 포도주는 그렇게 비싸지 않다고 생각하는데요.

   _____

3. 김미정 씨가 오늘 학교에 안 갔다고 생각합니다.

   _____

4. 제 아파트가 좀 불편하다고 생각합니다.

   _____

5. 그 영화가 재미있다고 생각하지 않습니다.

   _____

Adjectives: colors and
shapes in description

Stating reasons

Become/Get: adjective
stem + –어/아지다

Numbers from 100 to 1,000,00C

6. 이 책이 너무 길다고 생각합니다.

_____

7. 이 케이크가 너무 달다고 생각하지 않으세요?

_____

8. 그 카레는 안 맵다고 생각합니다.

_____

ANSWER KEY

1. *Do you think Mr.and Mrs. Lee are Chinese? 2. I think this wine is not so expensive. 3. I think Ms. Kim Mijeong didn't go to school today. 4. I think my apartment is a little inconvenient. 5. I don't think that movie is interesting. 6. I think this book is too long. 7. Don't you think this cake is too sweet? 8. I think that curry is not spicy.*

✎ Drive It Home

Fill in the blanks with appropriate words.

1. 슈퍼에 가서_____와 오이를 샀어요.

   I went to a supermarket and bought lettuce and cucumbers.

2. 한국에_____한국어를 일 년 동안 배웠어요.

   I went to Korea and studied Korean for a year.

3. 여섯 시 반에 일어났고, 아침을 먹었고, 신문을_____, 여덟 시에 집을 나가서
   회사에 갔어요.

   I woke up at six thirty, ate breakfast, read a newspaper, left home at eight, and went to work (lit: the company).

4. 열 두시까지 일하고 점심을_____한 시에 미팅에 참석해요.

   I work until twelve, eat lunch and attend the meeting at one.

5. 아주 맛있_____생각해요.

   I think it's very delicious.

6. 작년에 졸업_____ 생각합니다.

   I think he/she graduated last year.

7. 박지훈 씨가 오늘 바쁘_____생각해요?

   Do you think Mr. Park Ji-Hoon is busy today?

8. 로페즈 씨가 중국사람이 아니_____생각합니다.

   I think Ms. Lopez is not Chinese.

   ANSWER KEY
   1. 상추 2. 가서 3. 읽었고 4. 먹고 5. 다고 6. 했다고 7. 다고 8. 라고

How Did You Do?

Let's see how you did! By now, you should be able to:

☐ describe a sequence of events and actions. (Still unsure? Jump back to Grammar
  Builder 1.)

☐ state opinions with *I think that*. (Still unsure? Jump back to Grammar Builder 2.)

Don't forget to practice and reinforce what you've
learned by visiting **www.livinglanguage.com/
languagelab** for flashcards, games, and quizzes!

✎ Word Recall

   1. 외동딸   a. *five people*
   2. 다섯 명   b. *Is that so?*

Adjectives: colors and
shapes in description

Stating reasons

Become/Get: adjective
stem + –어/아지다

Numbers from 100 to 1,000,000

3. 외동아들	c. *I see.*
4. 그리고 나서	d. *family*
5. 그래요?	e. *only son*
6. 가족	f. *and then*
7. 그렇군요	g. *only daughter*
8. 얼굴	h. *It is spacious!*
9. 괜찮네!	i. *That is okay!*
10. 넓네!	j. *face*

ANSWER KEY
1. g; 2. a; 3. e; 4. f; 5. b; 6. d; 7. c; 8. j; 9. i; 10. h

Unit 1 Quiz

Let's put the most essential Korean words and grammar points you've learned so far to practice in the following exercises. It's important to be sure that you've mastered this material before you move on. Score the correct answers at the end of the unit quiz and see if you need to go back for more practice, or if you're ready to move on to Unit 2.

A. Fill in the blanks with adjectives in their appropriate form. Use polite endings unless specified otherwise.

1. 남동생 방이 _____?

   Is your younger brother's room clean?

   아니요, 별로 안_____.

   No, it isn't very clean.

2. 이 영화가 _____?

   Is this movie good?

   아니요,_____좋지 않아요.

   No, it isn't very good.

3. 그 피자가_____?

   Is that pizza delicious?

   아니요, 별로 _____.

   No, it isn't very delicious.

4. 그 백화점이_____?

   Is that department store famous?

아니요, 별로 _____

No, it isn't very famous. (long negation)

B. Fill in the blanks with adjectives and the verb *become*.

1. 7월이 되면 _____ .

   When July comes, it gets hot.

2. 제 컴퓨터가 _____ .

   My computer got old.

C. Fill in the blanks with the appropriate words + –어/아서.

1. 오늘은 비가 오고 춥고 게다가 바람이 불_____ 나가고 싶지 않아요.

   Today it's raining, cold, and furthermore, the wind is blowing, so I don't want to go out.

2. 제 아파트가 낡았고 게다가 역에서도 멀_____ 별로 좋지 않아요.

   My apartment is old, and furthermore, far from the station, so it's not so good.

D. Write the following numbers in Korean.

1. *773,823* _____

2. *859,754* _____

3. *999,999* _____

E. Complete the sentences using the appropriate words + the expression –네요. Pay attention to the tense.

1. 이 색깔은 너무 _____ .

   This color is too bright.

2. 그 영화가 너무 _____.

The movie is too short.

F. Fill in the blanks using the appropriate words + the indefinite pronoun 거.

1. 제 스웨터는 빨간색인데 영민 씨____는 파란색이에요.

My sweater is red but Mr. Young-min's is blue.

2. 이 비싼 스웨터는 예쁜데 그 싼____는 별로 안 예뻐요.

This expensive sweater is pretty but that cheap one is not very pretty.

G. Fill in the blanks with the appropriate verbs in their –고서 form.

1. 여섯 시에 일어나서 커피를_____신문을 읽어요.

I wake up at six, drink coffee, and read a newspaper.

2. 저녁을_____텔레비전을 보고 열 한시에 잠을 자요.

I eat dinner, watch TV, and go to sleep at eleven.

H. Fill in the blanks with the appropriate words + 다/라고 생각해요.

1. 이 씨가 미국인사람_____생각해요.

I think Mr. Lee is an American.

2. 이 스웨터는 안 싸_____생각해요.

I think this sweater is not cheap.

3. 이 후라이드 치킨은 맛있_____ 생각해요.

I think this fried chicken is delicious.

ANSWER KEY
A. 1. 깨끗해요, 깨끗해요 2. 좋아요, 별로 3. 맛있어요, 맛없어요 4. 유명해요, 유명하지 않아요
B. 1. 더워져요 2. 낡아졌어요
C. 1. 어서 2. 어서
D. 1. 칠십 칠만 삼천 팔백 이십 삼 2. 팔십 오만 구천 칠백 오십 사 3. 구십 구만 구천 구백 구십 구

E. 1. 밝네요 **2.** 짧네요
F. 1. 거 **2.** 거
G. 1. 마시고서 **2.** 먹고서
H. 1. 라고 **2.** 다고 **3.** 다고

How Did You Do?

Give yourself a point for every correct answer, then use the following key to tell whether you're ready to move on:

0–7 points: It's probably a good idea to go back through the lesson again. You may be moving too quickly, or there may be too much "down time" between your contact with Korean. Remember that it's better to spend 30 minutes with Korean three or four times a week than it is to spend two or three hours just once a week. Find a pace that's comfortable for you, and spread your contact hours out as much as you can.

8–12 points: You would benefit from a review before moving on. Go back and spend a little more time on the specific points that gave you trouble. Re-read the Grammar Builder sections that were difficult, and do the Work Outs one more time. Don't forget about the online supplemental practice material, either. Go to **www.livinglanguage.com/languagelab** for games and quizzes that will reinforce the material from this unit.

13–17 points: Good job! There are just a few points that you could consider reviewing before moving on. If you haven't worked with the games and quizzes on **www.livinglanguage.com/languagelab**, please give them a try.

18–20 points: Great! You're ready to move on to the next unit.

 **points**

Unit 2:
At a Restaurant

In Unit 2, you will learn the expressions you can use when dining out at a restaurant. You will also learn how to describe food. An honorific and a humble polite form of various verbs will also be introduced. By the end of the unit, you'll be able to use key vocabulary to talk about dining at a restaurant. You'll learn how to use giving and receiving verbs, as well as honorific and humble polite forms of verbs. You'll know how to express past experience, including using adjectives in their past tense forms and expressing *before* ... and *after* .... You'll also learn how to express past desires (*I wanted to* ...) and make suggestions (*Let's* ... , *Why don't we* ... ?, *Shall we* ... ?) Finally, you'll know how to express the conditional (*will do/ would do*). Ready to get started?

Lesson 5: Words
In this lesson you'll learn how to:

☐ use key vocabulary related to food and dining.

☐ use giving and receiving verbs.

☐ express a completion of an action and an attempt.

Giving and receiving
verbs

Adjectives: past status or condition

Expressing past
experience

Before and after: –기 전에 and
–ㄴ/은 후에

Word Builder 1

(▶) 5A Word Builder 1

두 분	two people (honorific)
비빔밥	bibimbop (rice bowl with vegetables and a spicy sauce)
김치	kimchi (spicy pickled cabbage)
갈비	marinated sweet ribs
불고기	sweet marinated grilled beef
삼겹살	grilled pork belly
냉면	cold broth noodle
된장	soybean paste
찌개	stew (style of food)
밥	cooked rice, meal
백반	meal with a bowl of rice, soup, and side dishes
음식	food
소스	sauce
양	amount
반	half
짠	salty
단	sweet
한번	once
주문하다	to order
주다	to give
받다	to receive
드시다	to eat, to drink (honorific)

Expressing desires: –고
싶었어요 (past tense)

–면 됩니다 (*will do/would do*)

Take It Further 1

▶ 5B Take It Further 1

The sharing of large dishes among guests of the same group is common in Korea, and for these sharing dishes, people commonly order one person's portion or two people's portion. For example, Koreans bring the barbecue inside of the dining hall and grill meats on the table inside of the restaurant. At such a restaurant, waitresses and waiters usually use 일 인분 (*one person's portion*), 이 인분 (*two people's portion*), 삼 인분 (*three people's portion*), 사 인분 (*four people's portion*), 오 인분 (*five people's portion*), and so on to take the orders.

✎ Word Practice 1

Translate the following words into Korean.

grilled pork belly	1.
cooked rice, meal	2.
meal with a bowl of rice, soup, and side dishes	3.
food	4.
amount	5.
half	6.
to give	7.
salty	8.
once	9.
to order	10.

ANSWER KEY
1. 삼겹살 2. 밥 3. 백반 4. 음식 5. 양 6. 반 7. 주다 8. 짠 9. 한번 10. 주문하다

Giving and receiving
verbs

Adjectives: past status or condition

Expressing past
experience

Before and *after*: –기 전에 and
–ㄴ/은 후에

Grammar Builder 1

▶ 5C Grammar Builder 1

GIVING AND RECEIVING VERBS

주다 (*to give*), 받다 (*to receive*), and 드리다 (*to give to an older person, honorific*) are called the giving and receiving verbs. With these verbs you will need to express "to someone" and "from someone" by choosing the appropriate particles.

주다 (*to give*) uses this [*to* + someone] structure. The particle used to represent *to* is 에게. 에게 is only used for humans or animals who are the receivers of an object.

마이클에게 책을 줘요.
I give a book to Michael.

언니에게 선물을 줬어요.
I gave a gift to my older sister.

학생들에게 한국어를 가르쳐 줬어요.
I taught Korean to students.

Another particle, 한테, is used in the same situation as 에게 but 한테 is used in more casual conversations.

동생한테 책을 줘요.
I give a book to my younger sibling.

개한테 밥을 줘요.
I give a meal to a dog.

에게 or 한테 have an honorific form –께. This form is used in a conversational context when speaking to an older person to whom you are giving an object.

olite expressions: honorific and
humble polite forms of verbs

Inviting people: *Let's ...* , *Why
don't we ... ?, Shall we ... ?*

Expressing desires: –고
싶었어요 (past tense)

–면 됩니다 (*will do/would do*)

이건 아버님께 드리는 선물입니다.
This is the gift that I give to father.

할머니께 이 우산을 갖다 드리세요.
Please give this umbrella to grandmother.

선생님께 빨리 가 보세요.
Please go to the teacher quickly.

The verb *to give* has two forms: One is the non-honorific form you've just seen,
주다, and the other is an honorific form: 드리다. Let's look at some examples
of the honorific form 드리다. Notice when you use 드리다 it is almost always
accompanied by the honorific particle 께.

크리스마스에 할아버지께 선물을 드렸습니다.
I gave a gift to grandfather on Christmas.

큰 아버지 생신에 온 가족이 큰 선물을 드릴 거예요.
*All the family members will give a big gift to uncle (lit: father's older brother) on his
birthday.*

보통 어머니께 스웨터를 사 드려요.
I usually buy and give a sweater to mother.

The verb *to receive* is 받다. This verb uses the particle 에게서 or 한테서, meaning
"*from (someone)*." 에게서 is a relatively formal form, while 한테서 is a relatively
informal form, just as 에게 and 한테 we learned earlier.

어제 어머니에게서 스카프를 받았어요.
I received a scarf from mother yesterday.

부모님에게서 비싼 카메라를 받았어요.

I received an expensive camera from my parents.

생일에는 여동생한테서 전화를 받아요.

On my birthday I receive a phone call from my younger sister.

제 남자친구한테서 초콜릿과 장미를 받았어요.

I received chocolates and roses from my boyfriend.

께 can also be used as an honorific form of *from* as shown in the examples below.

김 선생님께 사전을 받았어요.

I received a dictionary from Mr. Kim (lit: Professor Kim).

아버지께 책을 받았습니다.

I received a book from my father.

In these sentences, 께, which is an honorific form of 에게서/한테서 means *from*.

✎ Work Out 1

Fill in the blanks with the appropriate giving and receiving verbs listed below. Change them into their appropriate forms as necessary.

드릴 거예요, 주었어요, 받았어요, 사 드렸어요

1. 남동생에게 낡은 컴퓨터를_____.

   I gave my younger brother an old computer.

2. 김 선생님께 사전을_____.

   I received a dictionary from Mr. Kim.

3. 은숙 씨가 제 여동생에게 초콜릿을_____.

Ms. Eun-Sook gave my younger sister chocolates.

4. 저와 제 룸메이트가 내일 선생님께 꽃을_____.

My roommate and I will give our teacher flowers tomorrow.

5. 오랜 친구에게서 이 와인을_____.

I received this wine from my old friend.

6. 부모님께 비싼 카메라를_____.

I bought and gave an expensive camera to my parents.

ANSWER KEY
1. 줬어요 2. 받았어요 3. 줬어요 4. 드릴 거예요 5. 받았어요 6. 사 드렸어요

Word Builder 2

(▶) 5D Word Builder 2

생선 구이	*broiled fish*
생선 튀김	*fried fish*
나물	*cooked vegetable (side dish)*
새우	*shrimp*
오징어	*cuttlefish, squid*
문어	*octopus*
반찬	*side dish*
버섯	*mushroom*
전골	*hot pot*
스파게티	*spaghetti*
한식	*Korean-style/Korean-style food*
양식	*Western-style/Western-style food*
기회	*chance*

Giving and receiving
verbs

Adjectives: past status or condition

Expressing past
experience

Before and *after*: –기 전에 and
–ㄴ/은 후에

디저트	*dessert*
아이스크림	*ice cream*
치즈 케익	*cheesecake*
초콜릿 케익	*chocolate cake*
카푸치노	*cappuccino*
카페 오레	*café au lait*
사장님	*president of a company*
이사님	*division/regional manager*
부장님	*section manager*
찬	*cold*
드시다	*to eat, to drink (honorific)*
뵙다	*to see, to meet (humble)*

Take It Further 2

▶ 5E Take It Further 2

Note that –님 is attached to the job titles, kinship terms or people's names
to express politeness to the people being addressed in conversation. Some
examples of titles that use –님: 선생님 (*teacher*), 사모님 (*owner's wife/lady*),
은사님 (*teacher I am indebted to*), 고모님 (*someone's father's older sister*), 할머님
(*someone's grandmother*), 할아버님 (*someone's grandfather*), 아버님 (*someone's
father*), 변호사님 (*lawyer*), 교수님 (*professor*).

✎ Word Practice 2

Translate the following words or phrases into Korean.

| *fried fish* | 1. |
| *shrimp* | 2. |

olite expressions: honorific and
humble polite forms of verbs

Inviting people: *Let's* ... , *Why
don't we* ... ?, *Shall we* ... ?

Expressing desires: –고
싶었어요 (past tense)

–면 됩니다 (*will do/would do*)

cooked vegetable	3.
Korean-style/Korean-style food	4.
Western-style/Western-style food	5.
chance	6.
president of a company	7.
division/regional manager	8.
section manager	9.
mushroom	10.

ANSWER KEY
1. 생선 튀김 2. 새우 3. 나물 4. 한식 5. 양식 6. 기회 7. 사장님 8. 이사님 9. 부장님 10. 버섯

Grammar Builder 2

▶ 5F Grammar Builder 2

EXPRESSING PAST EXPERIENCE

We already learned that the simple past form in Korean is expressed with
–ㅆ/었/았 depending on the ending of the preceding words. To express
something that you experienced before, we will use the new form –ㄴ/은 적이
있어요. This is comparable to the present perfect in English (*have gone, have
seen*).

그 드라마를 본 적이 있어요?
Have you seen that drama?

아니오, 본 적이 없어요.
No, I haven't seen it.

전에 한국어를 배운 적이 있어요?
Have you learned Korean before?

Giving and receiving
verbs

Adjectives: past status or condition

Expressing past
experience

Before and *after*: –기 전에 and
–ㄴ/은 후에

When you want to talk about things you've tried in the past or ask someone else what they've tried before, use –어/아 본 적이 있어요. The negative form will be –어/아 본 적이 없어요.

한식을 먹어 본 적이 있어요?
Have you tried Korean-style food before?

사장님과 일해 본 적이 있어요?
Have you worked with our company's president?

스파게티를 만들어 본 적이 있어요?
Have you ever made spaghetti?

아니오, 만들어 본 적이 없어요.
No, I haven't made it.

그 음악을 들어 본 적이 있어요.
I have listened to that music.

✎ Work Out 2

Translate the following Korean sentences into English.

1. 김치찌개를 만들어 본 적이 있어요.

———————————————————————————————

2. 영미 씨는 정말 매운 음식을 먹어 본 적이 없어요.

———————————————————————————————

3. 이사님과 일해 본 적이 있어요?

———————————————————————————————

olite expressions: honorific and
humble polite forms of verbs

Inviting people: *Let's* ... , *Why
don't we* ... ?, *Shall we* ... ?

Expressing desires: –고
싶었어요 (past tense)

–면 됩니다 (*will do/would do*)

4. 스페인에 여행해 본 적이 있어요?

_____

5. 오징어 튀김을 먹어 본 적이 있어요?

_____

6. 생일에 예쁜 꽃을 받은 적이 있어요.

_____

ANSWER KEY

1. *I have made kimchi stew.* 2. *Ms. Youngmi has not tried really spicy food.* 3. *Have you worked with the regional manager?* 4. *Have you traveled to Spain?* 5. *Have you tried fried cuttlefish?* 6. *I have received pretty flowers on my birthday.*

✎ Drive It Home

A. Fill in the blanks by choosing appropriate verbs from the word list below. Some answers will be repeated.

주셨습니다, 드렸습니다, 주었습니다, 받았습니다

1. 아버지께 카드를 _____.

I give a card to my father.

2. 이 선생님께서 저에게 펜을 _____.

Mr. Yi gave me a pen.

3. 아버지께 책을 _____.

I received a book from my father.

4. 할아버지께서 어머니께 스웨터를 _____.

Grandfather gave mother a sweater.

5. 남동생이 저에게 책을 _____.

My younger brother gave me a book.

Giving and receiving
verbs

Adjectives: past status or condition

Expressing past
experience

Before and *after*: –기 전에 and
–ㄴ/은 후에

B. Fill in the blanks with expression of past experience –어/아 본 적이 있어요 or
–어/아 본 적이 없어요.

1. 아이스크림 튀김을 _____.

   I have tried fried ice cream.

2. 그 양식을 _____.

   I have not tried that Western-style food.

3. 그 음악을_____.

   I have listened to that music.

C. Fill in the blanks with appropriate particles.

1. 사장님_____이 커피를 드리세요.

   Please give this coffee to the company's president.

2. 할머니께서 저_____좋은 선물을 주셨어요.

   Grandmother gave a good gift to me.

3. 룸메이트가 내일 김 선생님_____꽃을 드릴 거예요.

   My roommate will give flowers to Mr. Kim.

ANSWER KEY
A. 1. 드렸습니다 2. 주셨습니다 3. 받았습니다 4. 주셨습니다 5. 주었습니다
B. 1. 먹어 본 적이 있어요 2. 먹어 본 적이 없어요 3. 들어본 적이 있어요
C. 1. 께 2. 에게 or 한테 3. 께

🌐 Culture Note

In Korean restaurants and cafés, the service you receive is generally good and
there is no need to leave any tip! When you are seated, you are immediately
served water and after you order the food, you would be served quickly compared
to most American kitchens. The waitresses or waiters do not come around often

Polite expressions: honorific and humble polite forms of verbs | Inviting people: *Let's ... , Why don't we ... ?, Shall we ... ?*

Expressing desires: –고 싶었어요 (past tense) | –면 됩니다 (*will do/would do*)

unless you flag them by hand or call them. Customers usually pay for their food at the cashier by bringing their own check after they are given it by the server.

How Did You Do?

Let's see how you did! By now, you should be able to:

☐ use key vocabulary related to food and dining. (Still unsure? Jump back to Word Builder 1 or Word Builder 2.)

☐ use giving and receiving verbs. (Still unsure? Jump back to Grammar Builder 1.)

☐ express past experience. (Still unsure? Jump back to Grammar Builder 2.)

✎ Word Recall

1. 가까운	a. *interesting*
2. 새로운	b. *far*
3. 재미있는	c. *difficult*
4. 어려운	d. *near*
5. 친절한	e. *delicious*
6. 맛없는	f. *boring*
7. 낮은	g. *new*
8. 맛있는	h. *low*
9. 재미없는	i. *kind*
10. 먼	j. *not delicious*

ANSWER KEY
1. d; 2. g; 3. a; 4. c; 5. i; 6. j; 7. h; 8. e; 9. f; 10. b

Giving and receiving
verbs

Adjectives: past status or condition

Expressing past
experience

Before and *after*: –기 전에 and
–ㄴ/은 후에

Lesson 6: Phrases

In this lesson you'll learn how to:

☐ use adjectives in the past tense.

☐ express *before* ... and *after* ...

Phrase Builder 1

▶ 6A Phrase Builder 1

예쁜 레스토랑	*pretty restaurant*
어떤 음식	*what kind of meal*
붐비다	*to be crowded*
코스 요리	*course meal*
한정식	*Korean-style full course meal*
커피나 그런 거	*coffee or something like that*
밥 위에	*on top of cooked rice*
나물이 밥 위에 얹혀 있는	*cooked vegetables are put on cooked rice*
사실	*actually*
나중에	*later*
레스토랑에서 나간 후	*after leaving a restaurant*
한정식으로 하겠습니다	*I will have a Korean-style full course meal*
그렇게 하세요	*please do so*
괜찮으시면	*if it's okay*
반을 주다	*to give half (non-honorific)*
반을 드리다	*to give half (honorific)*

Polite expressions: honorific and
humble polite forms of verbs

Inviting people: *Let's ... , Why
don't we ... ?, Shall we ... ?*

Expressing desires: –고
싶었어요 (past tense)

–면 됩니다 (*will do/would do*)

담배를 피우다	*to smoke*

Take It Further 1

▶ 6B Take It Further 1

When attached to a noun, –(이)나 means *or*. –(이)나 is used to indicate a disjunctive choice like *or* or *either A or B* in English. In the case of verb and adjective, use –거나. 그런 means *something like*. Therefore –(이)나 그런 is translated as *or something like that*.

커피나 그런 거
coffee or something like that

진수 씨나 그런 사람
Mr. Jinsoo or someone like him

–이 is added to 나 when the preceding noun ends with a consonant.

생선 튀김이나 그런 거
fried fish or something like that

Often this expression –(이)나 expresses an option (*or*) when offering someone a choice in a conversational context.

✎ Phrase Practice 1

Fill in the missing words below.

1. _____레스토랑

pretty restaurant

Giving and receiving
verbs

Adjectives: past status or condition

Expressing past
experience

Before and *after*: –기 전에 and
–ㄴ/은 후에

2. _____음식

what kind of meal

3. _____다

be crowded

4. _____식

Korean-style full course meal

5. 5. 커피_____그런 거

coffee or something like that

6. _____

actually

7. 한정식_____하겠습니다

will have a Korean-style full course meal

8. 8. 괜찮_____

if it's okay

ANSWER KEY
1. 예쁜 2. 어떤 3. 붐비 4. 한정 5. 나 6. 사실 7. 으로 8. 으시면

Grammar Builder 1

▶ 6C Grammar Builder 1

ADJECTIVES: PAST STATUS OR CONDITION

We have practiced present form of various adjectives in Unit 1. Now, let's learn their past tense form: adjective + –ㅆ/었/았 + 던. These forms are used to describe status or condition that happened in the past but the status or condition is often no longer true. In essence, it is similar to the English expression *used to* but can also be simply used as the past tense of adjectives like 좋은 (*good*): 좋았던.

PRESENT	PAST	PRESENT	PAST
무거운 *heavy*	무거웠던	가벼운 *light*	가벼웠던
긴 *long*	길었던	짧은 *short*	짧았던
좀 큰 *a little big*	좀 컸던	좁은 *narrow*	좁았던
더운 *warm (weather)*	더웠던	추운 *cold (weather)*	추웠던
따뜻한 *warm (object)*	따뜻했던	차가운 *cold (object)*	차가웠던
어두운 *dark*	어두웠던	밝은 *bright*	밝았던
맛있는 *delicious*	맛있었던	맛없는 *not tasty*	맛없었던
하얀 *white*	하얬던	까만 *black*	까맸던
깨끗한 *clean*	깨끗했던	조용한 *quiet*	조용했던
활발한 *lively*	활발했던	유명한 *famous*	유명했던
비싼 *expensive*	비쌌던	싼 *cheap*	쌌던
편리한 *convenient*	편리했던	불편한 *inconvenient*	불편했던
좋은 *good*	좋았던	나쁜 *bad*	나빴던

Giving and receiving
verbs

Adjectives: past status or condition

Expressing past
experience

Before and *after*: –기 전에 and
–ㄴ/은 후에

PRESENT	PAST	PRESENT	PAST
시원한 *cool*	시원했던	부족한 *insufficient*	부족했던
매운 *spicy*	매웠던	짠 *salty*	짰던
재미있는 *interesting*	재미있었던	재미없는 *uninteresting*	재미없었던
친절한 *kind*	친절했던	불친절한 *unkind*	불친절했던

Let's look at some phrases using –ㅆ/었/았던.

정말 맛있었던 한정식집

the Korean-style full course meal restaurant that used to be so delicious

아주 매웠던 한국 음식

the Korean food that was very spicy

음악이 좋았던 카페

the café where music was great

아주 추웠던 어느 날

one day that was really cold

엘레베이터가 없어서 불편했던 빌딩

the building that did not have an elevator, so was inconvenient

아주 달았던 케잌

the cake that was very sweet

열 사람한테는 부족했던 음식

the food that was insufficient for ten people

Polite expressions: honorific and
humble polite forms of verbs

Inviting people: *Let's ... , Why
don't we ... ?, Shall we ... ?*

Expressing desires: –고
싶었어요 (past tense)

–면 됩니다 (*will do/would do*)

재미있었던 영화

the movie that was interesting/funny

Now let's practice these past adjectival phrases in longer sentences along with other phrases.

미국에서는 먹을 수 없었던 매운 갈비가 서울에서는 인기가 많았습니다.

The spicy rib that I couldn't eat/couldn't get in the U.S. was popular in Seoul.

아주 복잡하고 사람이 많았던 명동에 다시 가고 싶습니다.

I would like to go back to Myong-Dong, which was very crowded and had many people.

가격이 쌌던 한정식집이었는데 맛은 아주 좋았습니다.

The prices at the Korean-style full course meal restaurant were cheap, yet the food was very tasty.

낮에는 조용했던 술집들이 밤에는 아주 시끄럽습니다.

The bars that were quiet during the day are very noisy at night.

친절했던 점원이 잘 설명해 주었어요.

The clerk that was kind explained it well.

✎ Work Out 1

Fill in the blanks with the appropriate form of the adjectives below.

어려웠던, 달았던, 붐볐던, 컸던, 불편했던

1. _____가게가 편리하게 바뀌었어요.

The store that used to be inconvenient has changed into a convenient store.

2. 아침에는_____도서관이 오후에 붐볐습니다.

The library that was quiet in the morning got crowded in the afternoon.

3. 갈비가 아주_____음식점이었습니다.

It used to be a restaurant that had very sweet ribs.

4. 그 전에는_____빌딩이 작게 보였습니다.

The building that used to be big before looked small.

5. _____인터뷰가 끝나고 우리 모두 맛있는 한정식 집으로 갔습니다.

After the difficult interview was over, all of us went to the delicious Korean-style full course meal restaurant.

ANSWER KEY

1. 불편했던 2. 조용했던 3. 달았던 4. 컸던 5. 어려웠던

Phrase Builder 2

▶ 6D Phrase Builder 2

그 생선 요리	*that fish dish*
이 멕시코 샐러드	*this Mexican salad*
그 홍합 요리	*that mussel dish*
디저트나 커피 그런 거	*dessert or coffee or something like that*
어떠셨어요?	*How was it? (honorific)*
어땠어요?	*How was it?*
한번 와서 먹어보고 싶었어요	*I wanted to come and try (to eat) once*
어떤지 한번 봅시다.	*Let's try seeing how it is.*
기회가 없었어요	*I didn't have an opportunity*
홍합도 더해졌어요	*mussels are also added to it*
양이 많았어요	*it was a lot (lit: the amount was a lot)*

전부 다 먹었어요	I finished eating everything
술을 너무 마셨어요	I drank too much
적게 먹었어요	I ate a little
좀 더 드실래요?	Would you like to eat/drink a little more? (honorific polite)
호텔 근처에	near the hotel
이사님을 뵈다	to meet a regional manager (humble)
이사님을 뵈었을 때 (past tense)	when I met a division manager (humble)
한번 더	one more time
커피면 됩니다	I am okay with only coffee
그런 이유로	so, for that reason
물론	of course
기꺼이	gladly, willingly

✎ Phrase Practice 2

Fill in the missing words below.

1. _____어요?

How was it? (honorific)

2. _____어요?

How was it?

3. 한번_____먹어보고 싶었어요.

I wanted to come and try (to eat).

4. 어떤지_____봅시다

Let's try seeing how it is.

Giving and receiving
verbs

Adjectives: past status or condition

Expressing past
experience

Before and *after*: –기 전에 and
–ㄴ/은 후에

5. _____ 없었어요.

I didn't have an opportunity.

6. _____ 먹었어요.

I ate a little.

7. 한번_____

one more time

8. 커피_____ 됩니다.

I am okay with only coffee.

ANSWER KEY
1. 어떠셨 2. 어땠 3. 와서 4. 한번 5. 기회가 6. 적게 7. 더 8. 면

Grammar Builder 2
▶ 6E Grammar Builder 2

BEFORE AND *AFTER*: –기 전에 AND –ㄴ/은 후에

You can describe a sequence of events or actions using 전 (*before*) and 후 (*after*).
전에 is preceded by –기, and 후에 is preceded by –ㄴ/은. –기 is a normalizer,
which means verb stem + 기 makes a verb a noun class, similar to how *–ing* is used
in English. –ㄴ/은 후에 behaves similarly to adjectives.

파티하기 전에 와인 두 병을 샀어요.
I bought two bottles of wine before having the party.

파티한 후에 방이 깨끗하지 않네요.
After having the party the room is not clean.

저녁 먹기 전에 숙제를 했어요.
I did my homework before eating dinner.

Expressing desires: –고
싶었어요 (past tense)

–면 됩니다 (*will do/would do*)

저녁 먹은 후에 숙제를 했어요.
I did my homework after eating dinner.

미팅하기 전에 점심을 먹었어요.
Before having the meeting, I ate lunch.

미팅한 후에 점심을 먹었어요.
After having the meeting, I ate lunch.

영화를 보기 전에 표를 샀어요.
We bought tickets before watching the movie.

영화를 본 후에 친구들과 이야기를 했어요.
My friends and I talked after seeing the movie.

은행에서 일하기 전에 회사에서 일했어요.
Before working at the bank I worked for a company.

시험 보기 전에 공부를 많이 했어요.
Before taking a test I studied a lot.

운동을 한 후 물을 많이 마셨어요.
After exercising I drank a lot of water.

기차를 탄 후 버스를 다시 탔어요.
After riding a train I rode a bus again.

Note that –기 only accepts verb infinitives.

Giving and receiving
verbs

Adjectives: past status or condition

Expressing past
experience

Before and *after*: –기 전에 and
–ㄴ/은 후에

✎ Work Out 2

Fill in the blanks with the appropriate Korean expressions.

1. 저녁을_____친구에게 전화할게요.

   I will call my friend before eating dinner.

2. _____커피를 마셔요.

   I drink coffee after getting up.

3. 한국에_____전에 한국어를 공부했어요.

   I studied Korean before going to Korea.

4. 점심을 먹은_____카페에 갔어요.

   I went to a café after having lunch.

5. _____전에 책을 읽어요.

   I read a book before going to bed.

6. 커피를_____후에 디저트를 먹었어요.

   We ate dessert after drinking coffee.

   ANSWER KEY
   1. 먹기 전에 2. 일어난 후에 3. 가기 4. 후에 5. 자기 6. 마신

✎ Drive It Home

A. Fill in the blanks with the appropriate form of the adjectives based on the English
   translations.

1. _____책을 다 읽었어요.

   I finished reading a book that was difficult.

Expressing desires: –고
싶었어요 (past tense)

–면 됩니다 (*will do/would do*)

2. 그 집 음식이_____생각이 납니다.

I think the food at that restaurant was delicious.

3. 10년 전에_____나무가 이제는 아주 커졌습니다.

The tree that used to be small ten years ago now became very big.

4. 한국에서 아주_____고추장이 지금은 맵지 않습니다.

The red pepper paste that was very spicy to me in Korea is not spicy now.

5. 지난 금요일에_____꽃이 이제는 예쁘지 않습니다.

The flowers that were pretty last Friday are no longer pretty now.

B. Fill in the blanks with the appropriate words to complete the sentences.

1. 파티하기_____와인을 샀습니다.

I bought wine before having the party.

2. _____후에 와인을 샀습니다.

I bought wine after having the party.

3. 미팅_____점심을 먹었습니다.

After the meeting, I ate lunch.

4. 미팅에_____후에 점심을 먹었습니다.

After attending the meeting, I ate lunch.

5. _____후에 같이 저녁을 먹으러 갑시다.

After working, let's go to eat dinner together.

ANSWER KEY
A. 1. 어려웠던 2. 맛있었던 3. 작았던 4. 매웠던 5. 예뻤던
B. 1. 전에 2. 파티한 3. 후에 4. 참석한 5. 일한

Giving and receiving
verbs

Adjectives: past status or condition

Expressing past
experience

Before and *after*: –기 전에 and
–ㄴ/은 후에

Tip!

Keeping a diary in Korean is a good way to improve your Korean language skills. You can write about things you do and experience every day using several sentences you already know. Challenge yourself by going beyond simple sentences; try putting together more complex sentences using structures such as past adjectives (–ㅆ/았/었던), –면 conditionals, –기 전에 (*before*), –ㄴ/은 후에 (*after*), as well as conjunctions such as –고 *and*, –지만 *although*, –어/아서 *because*, and –기 때문에 *because*.

How Did You Do?

Let's see how you did! By now, you should be able to:

☐ use adjectives in their past tense forms. (Still unsure? Jump back to Grammar Builder 1.)

☐ express *before* … and *after* … (Still unsure? Jump back to Grammar Builder 2.)

✎ Word Recall

1. 모	a. *wool*
2. 현금	b. *cash*
3. 셔츠	c. *store clerk*
4. 바지	d. *popularity*
5. 거스름돈	e. *design*
6. 인기	f. *shirt*
7. 점원	g. *pants*
8. 줄무늬	h. *skirt*
9. 치마	i. *change*
10. 디자인	j. *stripes*

ANSWER KEY
1. a; 2. b; 3. f; 4. g; 5. i; 6. d; 7. c; 8. j; 9. h; 10. e

Lesson 7: Sentences

In this lesson you'll learn how to:

☐ use honorific and humble polite forms of verbs.

☐ express *wanted to ...*

Sentence Builder 1

⊳ 7A Sentence Builder 1

이 레스토랑이 아주 인기가 많아서 항상 붐벼요.	*This restaurant is very popular, so it's always crowded.*
뭐 드시겠습니까 ?	*What would you like to eat?*
이 식당이 갈비가 맛있는지 모르겠네요.	*I wonder if galbi is delicious at this restaurant.*
비빔밥이 어떤 음식이에요 ?	*What kind of meal is bibimbop?*
매운 소스와 나물이 밥 위에 얹혀 있는 음식이에요.	*It's cooked vegetables with a spicy sauce placed over cooked rice.*
지난 주에 여기서 비빔밥을 먹었는데 아주 맛있었어요.	*I ate bibimbop here last week, and it was very delicious.*
한번 드셔 보세요.	*Try it once. (lit: Eat it once.)*
그럼 오늘은 비빔밥으로 하겠습니다.	*Then today I will have bibimbop. (lit: I will do with bibimbop.)*
샐러드도 주문할까요?	*Shall I order a salad, too?*
괜찮으시면 제 것 반을 드릴게요.	*If it's okay with you, I will give you half of mine.*

Giving and receiving
verbs

Adjectives: past status or condition

Expressing past
experience

Before and *after*: –기 전에 and
–ㄴ/은 후에

지난 주에 샐러드를 주문했을때 양이 많았어요.	When I ordered a salad last week, it was quite large (lit: the amount was a lot).
여기는 붐비니까 나중에 카페로 가요.	It's crowded here, so afterwards let's go to a café.
시간이 있으면 이 레스토랑에서 나간 후 카페에서 커피나 그런 거를 마시는 게 어떻겠어요?	If we have time, after leaving this restaurant, how about we have coffee or something like that at a café?
그럼 주문할까요?	Shall we order then ?
네, 주문해요!	Yes, let's order!

✎ Sentence Practice 1

Fill in the missing words in each of the following sentences.

1. 이 레스토랑이 아주 인기가 많아서 항상_____.

   This restaurant is very popular, so it's always crowded.

2. 비빔밥이_____음식이에요?

   What kind of meal is bibimbop?

3. 한번_____보세요.

   Try it once. (lit: Eat it once.)

4. 그럼 오늘은_____하겠습니다.

   Then today I will have bibimbop. (lit: I will do with bibimbop.)

5. 시간이 있으면 이 레스토랑에서_____후 카페에서 커피나 그런 거를 마시는 게 어떻겠어요?

polite expressions: honorific and
humble polite forms of verbs

Inviting people: *Let's ...* , *Why
don't we ... ?*, *Shall we ... ?*

Expressing desires: –고
싶었어요 (past tense)

–면 됩니다 (*will do/would do*)

*If we have time, after leaving this restaurant, why don't we have coffee or something
like that at a café?*

6. 그럼_____할까요?

Shall we order then?

7. 네, 주문_____!

Yes, let's order!

ANSWER KEY
1. 붐벼요 2. 어떤 3. 드셔 4. 비빔밥으로 5. 나간 6. 주문 7. 해요

Grammar Builder 1
▶ 7B Grammar Builder 1

POLITE EXPRESSIONS: HONORIFIC AND HUMBLE POLITE
FORMS OF VERBS

You were already introduced to some polite expressions in *Intermediate Korean*.
Now, let's look at the humble forms of pronouns and verbs. Not all Korean words
have humble forms, but some do; if they have a humble form, you're supposed
to use them to be polite in social situations. Let's take a look at some of the
pronouns. Notice that you humble yourself and your group of people but you
don't humble the 2nd person or 3rd persons.

BASE FORM	HUMBLE FORM
나 *I*	저
나의 *my*	제
우리 *we*	저희

Giving and receiving
verbs

Adjectives: past status or condition

Expressing past
experience

Before and after: –기 전에 and
–ㄴ/은 후에

BASE FORM	HUMBLE FORM
우리의 *our*	저희

Let's take a look at some honorific forms of verbs. Not all verbs have special honorific and humble forms; in cases where a honorific form isn't available, the subject-honorific form can be formed using the –시 in front of the sentence ending.

BASE FORM	HONORIFIC FORM
먹다 *to eat*	드시다 *to eat food or to drink*
먹다 *to eat*	잡수시다 *to eat a meal*
자다 *to sleep*	주무시다
죽다 *to die*	돌아가시다
있다 *to be/to stay*	계시다
말하다 *to speak*	말씀하시다

To form an honorific verb, use –시 as you can see in the following chart.

BASE FORM	HONORIFIC FORM
보다 *to see*	보시다
만나다 *to meet*	만나시다
주다 *to give*	주시다

Expressing desires: –고
싶었어요 (past tense)

–면 됩니다 (*will do/would do*)

BASE FORM	HONORIFIC FORM
가다 *to go*	가시다
오다 *to come*	오시다
읽다 *to read*	읽으시다
이다 *to be*	이시다

As you saw in 읽으시다, a dummy vowel 으 is added if the verb stem ends with a
consonant. Lastly, let's take a look at a list of honorific nouns. Some of them you
will recognize from *Intermediate Korean*.

BASE FORM	HONORIFIC FORM
나이 *age*	연세
딸 *daughter*	따님
이름 *name*	성함
사람/명 *person, people*	분
생일 *birthday*	생신
집 *home, house*	댁
밥 *rice, meal*	진지
말 *words, speech*	말씀

Now, let's look at how the honorific and humble polite forms of verbs are used.
As pointed out in *Intermediate Korean*, an honorific form is used when describing

Giving and receiving
verbs

Adjectives: past status or condition

Expressing past
experience

Before and *after*: −기 전에 and
−ㄴ/은 후에

actions taken by someone you need to or want to pay respect to in social relations, such as a superior at work, a teacher or a customer. On the other hand, a humble form is used when describing actions taken by the speaker himself/herself or members of his/her inner group, such as a family member. Let's take a look at mini-dialogue between 사장님 (*president of a company*) and 직원 (*employee*) whose name is 김현식.

사장님: 내일 언제 옵니까?
When are you coming tomorrow?

직원: 여덟 시 반쯤 옵니다. 사장님께서는요?
About eight thirty, I will come. How about you, Mr. Company's President?

사장님: 나는 한 아홉 시쯤.
As for me, about nine.

직원: 댁이 머세요?
Is your house far?

사장님: 좀 먼데, 김현식 씨 집은 가까워요?
A little bit far, but is your house close, Mr. Kim Hyun-Shik?

직원: 네, 저도 집이 별로 가깝지는 않습니다.
No, as for me, our home is not that close either.

사장 used shorter sentences overall because he does not need to place all the honorific grammar forms at the end of his sentences since his speech is directed to a person of lower status in the company. Meanwhile, the 직원 is using all the honorific and polite forms in his sentences; also his word choice is 댁 when referring to the 사장님's house. Notice that when he refers to his own house, he switches the word to 집.

olite expressions: honorific and
humble polite forms of verbs

Inviting people: *Let's ... , Why
don't we ... ?, Shall we ... ?*

Expressing desires: –고
싶었어요 (past tense)

–면 됩니다 (*will do/would do*)

🌐 Culture Note

When speaking Korean, you don't call a respected person directly by their name
in a conversation. It is a social convention in Korea to call a respected person
by his or her title instead. Traditionally, using the name of a respected person
(a nobleman) was forbidden, as a personal name was considered that person's
sacred property. "Calling names" directly was considered to be the actions of a
menial person and the respected person or a nobleman should not be called by
his or her name. The nobleman had numerous nicknames invited by his family
when a name was needed for daily usage. Often these names came from features
of nature, such as *calm pond* (정호) or *white pine trees* (백송).

✎ Work Out 1

A. Choose the appropriate honorific polite form from the list below to complete the
sentences. Change them into their appropriate form if necessary.
치시다, 쓰시다, 보시다, 오시다, 드시다

1. 백 선생님께서 이 책을_____.

   Mr. Baek wrote this book.

2. 이사님께서 내일 미국에_____.

   The regional manager will come to the U.S.A. tomorrow.

3. 사장님께서 녹차를 좋아하시니까 많이_____.

   The president likes green tea, so I think he/she'll drink a lot.

4. 부장님께서 주말에 테니스를_____.

   The section manager plays tennis on weekends.

5. 선생님, 이 영화를_____?

   Teacher, did you see this movie?

B. Choose the appropriate humble form from the list below to complete the sentences.

제, 저는, 저희, 제가

1. 이사님, _____하겠습니다.

   Regional Manager, I'll do it.

2. 이 분은_____어머니세요.

   This person is our mother.

3. 사장님, 이 사람이_____아내입니다.

   President, this is my wife.

4. 부장님, _____대학을 미국에서 다녔습니다.

   Section manager, I went to a college in the U.S.

ANSWER KEY
A. 1. 쓰셨습니다 2. 오십니다 3. 드실 거예요 4. 치십니다 5. 보셨습니까
B. 1. 제가 2. 저희 3. 제 4. 저는

Sentence Builder 2

▶ 7C Sentence Builder 2

그 생선요리는 어떠셨어요?	*How was that fish dish? (polite)*
그 찌개 요리는 어떠셨어요?	*How was that stew dish?*
이 한식 백반도 좋습니다.	*This Korean-style meal with a bowl of rice, soup, and side dishes was also good.*
이 레스토랑에 한 번 와 보고 싶었어요.	*I wanted to come and try this restaurant once.*
여러 가지 재료 중에 새우, 오징어, 홍합이 많았는데 저는 다 먹었습니다.	*Among many ingredients, shrimp, cuttlefish, and mussels were in it, and there were a lot, but I finished it all.*
그리고 김종익 씨 요리도 좀 먹어서 . . .	*I also had a little bit of Mr. Kim Jong-Ik's dish, so . . .*

Polite expressions: honorific and
humble polite forms of verbs

Inviting people: *Let's ... , Why
don't we ... ?, Shall we ... ?*

Expressing desires: –고
싶었어요 (past tense)

–면 됩니다 (*will do/would do*)

와인 좀 더 드실래요?	Would you like to have a little more wine?
사실 어제 술을 너무 많이 마셨어요.	Actually, I drank too much yesterday.
이한일 이사님을 뵈었을 때 맥주 상품권을 주셨어요.	When I saw the Regional Manager Yi Han-Il, he gave me a beer gift certificate.
그래서 호텔 근처에서 맥주 열 병을 사서 다 마시게 되었어요.	So, I bought ten bottles of beer near the hotel and ended up drinking them all. (lit: became drinking them all)
디저트하고 커피나 그런 거를 주문하는게 어때요?	Why don't we order a dessert and coffee or something like that?
찬 디저트틀 먹고 싶네요.	I want to eat a cold dessert.
메뉴를 한번 더 봅시다.	Let's look at the menu one more time.
케익만 있네요.	There are only cakes.
아이스크림을 먹고 싶었는데요.	I wanted to eat ice cream.
저는 커피면 됩니다.	I'm fine with only coffee.
저는 초콜릿 케익하고 차로 하지요.	I will have chocolate cake and tea. (lit: I will do it with chocolate cake and tea.)

✎ Sentence Practice 2

Fill in the missing words in each of the following sentences.

1. 그 찌개_____어떠셨어요?

   How was that stew dish? (polite)

2. 이 한식_____좋습니다.

   This Korean-style meal with a bowl of rice, soup, and side dishes was also good.

Giving and receiving
verbs

Adjectives: past status or condition

Expressing past
experience

Before and *after*: –기 전에 and
–ㄴ/은 후에

3. 이 레스토랑에 한 번 와_____싶었어요.

   I wanted to come and try this restaurant once.

4. 와인_____더 드실래요?

   Would you like to have a little more wine?

5. 디저트하고 커피나_____거를 주문하는게 어때요?

   Why don't we order a dessert and coffee or something like that?

6. 메뉴를 한번 더_____.

   Let's look at the menu one more time.

7. _____있네요.

   There are only cakes.

8. 저는 _____됩니다.

   I'm fine with only coffee.

   ANSWER KEY
   1. 요리는 2. 백반도 3. 보고 4. 좀 5. 그런 6. 봅시다 7. 케익만 8. 커피면

Grammar Builder 2

▶ 7D Grammar Builder 2

EXPRESSING DESIRES: –고 싶었어요 (PAST TENSE)

In *Intermediate Korean*, the present tense form of –고 싶어요 (*want to*) was
introduced. Now let's learn the past tense form of –고 싶다.

이 레스토랑에 한번 와 보고 싶었어요.
I wanted to come to this restaurant once.

Expressing desires: –고 싶었어요 (past tense)

–면 됩니다 (*will do/would do*)

그 음식을 한번 먹어 보고 싶었는데, 잘 됐군요.
I have (always) wanted to try that food so it's great.

저는 디저트로 커피를 마시고 싶었는데 그 식당에 커피가 없었어요.
I wanted to drink coffee for dessert but that restaurant did not have coffee.

회색 스웨터를 사고 싶었지만 없어서 갈색을 샀어요.
I wanted to buy a gray sweater, but they didn't have one, so I bought a brown one.

Negate –고 싶다 by using the long negation form, –고 싶지 않다.

공부를 12시까지 하고 싶지 않아요.
I don't want to study until 12 o'clock.

공부를 12시까지 하고 싶지 않았어요.
I didn't want to study until 12 o'clock.

Another negative expression of desire –고 싶다 is expressed using –기 싫다.
The past tense of this form will be –기 싫었어요. Some examples of this negative
expression are below.

어제 청소하기 싫었지만 손님이 오셔서 청소를 해야 됐어요.
I didn't want to clean yesterday but guests were coming so I needed to clean.

대학을 졸업하고 바로 일하기 싫었어요. 그래서 한 달 동안 여행을 갔어요.
*I didn't want to work immediately after graduating from college. So I traveled for a
month.*

하얀 차를 또 사기 싫었어요. 그래서 까만 차를 샀어요.
I didn't want to buy a white car again. So I bought a black car.

✎ Work Out 2

Fill in the blanks with the appropriate expressions to complete the sentences.

1. 어제는 생선을 먹고_____오늘은 고기를 먹고 싶네요.

   I wanted to eat fish yesterday, but today I want to eat meat.

2. 일요일에 테니스를 치고_____월요일에 시험이 있어서 집에서 공부했어요.

   I wanted to play tennis on Sunday, but since there was a test on Monday, I studied at home.

3. 그 영화를 보고_____. 이 영화는 보기 싫었어요.

   I wanted to see that movie; I didn't want to see this movie.

4. 너무 더워서 남부에는 가기_____. 그래서 북부로 갔어요.

   Because it was very hot I did not want to go south. So I went north.

5. 이 책이 너무 길고 재미없어서 읽기가_____. 하지만 다 읽었어요.

   This book was too long and boring, so I didn't want to read it. However, I read it all.

ANSWER KEY
1. 싶었는데 2. 싶었는데 3. 싶었어요 4. 싫었어요 5. 싫었어요

✎ Drive It Home

A. Fill in the blanks by choosing the appropriate words from the word list below.
   마셔요, 나가요, 나가십니다, 드십니다

1. 이사님께서_____.

   The regional manager is going out.

2. 저는_____.

   I'm going out.

Polite expressions: honorific and
humble polite forms of verbs

Inviting people: *Let's … , Why
don't we … ?, Shall we … ?*

Expressing desires: –고
싶었어요 (past tense)

–면 됩니다 (*will do/would do*)

3. 이사님께서 맥주를_____.

   The regional manager drinks beer.

4. 제가 맥주를_____.

   I drink beer.

B. Fill in the blanks with the appropriate words.

1. 맥주를_____싶었어요.

   I wanted to drink beer.

2. 맥주를 마시기_____.

   I didn't want to drink beer.

3. 오징어를 먹고_____.

   I wanted to eat squid.

4. 오징어를 먹고 싶지_____.

   I didn't want to eat squid.

ANSWER KEY
A. 1. 나가십니다 2. 나가요 3. 드십니다 4. 마셔요
B. 1. 마시고 2. 싫었어요 3. 싶었어요 4. 않았어요

☀ Tip!

Korean food is getting more of a name for itself around the world. The popularity
of the signature Korean side dish, kimchi, has recently spread to Japan, China, and
many other Asian regions. The sweetly marinated meats such as galbi or bulgogi are
well-known and well-liked in the United States. There are many Korean restaurants
in larger cities around the world. If there's one in your town, visit it and see if you
can read the names of dishes—which will probably be written in both Korean and
English—in Korean. Also, try ordering your food in Korean. Maybe you can even
have a little chat with Korean waiters and waitresses!

How Did You Do?

Let's see how you did! By now, you should be able to:

☐ use honorific and humble forms of words. (Still unsure? Jump back to Grammar Builder 1.)

☐ express *wanted to* ... (Still unsure? Jump back to Grammar Builder 2.)

✎ Word Recall

1. 따뜻한	a. *bright*
2. 빌리다	b. *1,000 won*
3. 밝은	c. *to borrow*
4. 만원	d. *warm*
5. 가벼운	e. *white*
6. 하얀	f. *10,000 won*
7. 찾다	g. *light*
8. 천원	h. *to be hot*
9. 생각하다	i. *to look for*
10. 덥다	j. *to think*

ANSWER KEY
1. d; 2. c; 3. a; 4. f; 5. g; 6. e; 7. i; 8. b; 9. j; 10. h

Lesson 8: Conversations

In this lesson you'll learn how to:

☐ express *Let's* ... , *Why don't we* ... ?, *Shall we* ... ?

☐ express ... *would do*.

olite expressions: honorific and
humble polite forms of verbs

Inviting people: *Let's … , Why
don't we … ?, Shall we … ?*

Expressing desires: –고
싶었어요 (past tense)

–면 됩니다 (*will do/would do*)

◀ Conversation 1

▶ 8A Conversation 1

Ms. Taylor is having lunch with her Korean colleague Ms. Hyun-Ok at a Korean restaurant.

웨이터:	어서 오세요. 두 분이세요?
현옥:	네.
웨이터:	담배 피우세요?
현옥:	아니요.
웨이터:	그럼 이쪽으로 오세요. 여기 메뉴가 있습니다.
테일러:	작지만 예쁜 레스토랑이네요?
현옥:	네, 이 레스토랑이 아주 인기가 많아서 항상 붐벼요. 테일러 씨는 뭐 드시겠어요?
테일러:	이 식당이 갈비가 맛있는지 모르겠네요.
현옥:	비빔밥은 (테일러씨에게) 맛있을지/어떨지 모르겠네요.
테일러:	비빔밥이 어떤 음식이에요?
현옥:	매운 소스와 나물이 밥 위에 얹혀 있는 음식이에요. 사실 지난 주에 여기서 비빔밥을 먹었는데 아주 맛있었어요. 한번 드셔 보세요.
테일러:	네, 그럼 오늘은 비빔밥으로 할게요/할래요.
현옥:	저는 오늘 한식 코스 정식으로 할래요/할게요. 비빔밥은 코스 요리가 아니니까 샐러드를 주문하시는게 어때요?
테일러:	네, 좋은 생각이시네요.
현옥:	아참, 괜찮으시면 샐러드는 제 거 반을 드릴게요. 지난 주에 샐러드를 주문했는데 양이 꽤 많았어요.
테일러:	네, 그럼 그렇게 할게요. 음료수도 주문하실 거예요?
현옥:	글쎄요, 시간이 있으면 이 레스토랑에서 나간 후 카페에서 커피나 그런 거를 마시는게 어떻겠어요?
테일러:	그렇군요. 여기는 붐비니까 나중에 카페로 가요/가죠.
현옥:	그럼 주문할까요?
테일러:	네, 주문해요.

Giving and receiving
verbs

Adjectives: past status or condition

Expressing past
experience

Before and *after*: –기 전에 and
–ㄴ/은 후에

Waiter:	Welcome. Two people?
Hyun-Ok:	Yes.
Waiter:	Do you (lit: will you) smoke?
Hyun-Ok:	No.
Waiter:	Then, come this way, please. Here is the menu.
Taylor:	It's a small but pretty restaurant, isn't it?
Hyun-Ok:	Yes. This restaurant is very popular, so it's always crowded. What do you want to eat, Ms. Taylor?
Taylor:	Well, I wonder if galbi is delicious at this restaurant.
Hyun-Ok:	I wonder how you'd like the bibimbop.
Taylor:	What kind of dish is bibimbop?
Hyun-Ok:	It's cooked vegetables with a spicy sauce placed over cooked rice. Actually, I ate bibimbop here last week, and it was very delicious. Try it once.
Taylor:	Yes, then I will have bibimbop today.
Hyun-Ok:	I will have the Korean course meal today. Since bibimbop is not a course meal, how about ordering a salad?
Taylor:	Yes, I think it is a good idea.
Hyun-Ok:	Oh by the way, as for the salad, if it's okay with you, I'll give you half of mine. When I ordered the salad last week, it was pretty big.
Taylor:	Yes, then I will do so. Are we going to order drinks, too?
Hyun-Ok:	Well, if we have time, after (lit: we leave) the restaurant, why don't we have coffee or something like that at a café?
Taylor:	I see. It's crowded here, so let's go to a café later.
Hyun-Ok:	Shall we order then?
Taylor:	Yes, let's order.

olite expressions: honorific and
humble polite forms of verbs

Inviting people: *Let's …, Why
don't we … ?, Shall we … ?*

Expressing desires: –고
싶었어요 (past tense)

–면 됩니다 (*will do/would do*)

✎ Conversation Practice 1

Fill in the blanks in the following sentences with the missing words. If you're
unsure of the answer, listen to the conversation one more time.

1. 이 레스토랑이 인기가 많아서_____붐벼요.

2. 사실 지난 주에 여기서 비빔밥을_____아주 맛있었어요.

3. 비빔밥은 코스 요리가_____샐러드를 주문하시는게 어때요?

4. 아참,_____샐러드는 제 거 반을 드릴게요.

5. 시간이 있으면 이 레스토랑에서_____후 카페에서 커피나 그런 거를 하시는게

어떻겠어요?

ANSWER KEY
1. 항상 2. 먹었는데 3. 아니니까 4. 괜찮으시면 5. 나간

Grammar Builder 1

▶ 8B Grammar Builder 1

INVITING PEOPLE: *LET'S … , WHY DON'T WE … ?, SHALL WE … ?*

You already learned how to say *Let's …* and *Why don't we … ?* in *Intermediate
Korean*. Let's review these expressions as well as adding the expression *Shall we
…?*

Conjunctive form of the verb + 게 어때요?	*Why don't we … ?*
Conjunctive form of the verb + ㄹ/을까요?	*Shall we … ?*
Conjunctive form of the verb + –ㅂ시다	*Let's … !* (at least two speakers)

Giving and receiving
verbs   Adjectives: past status or condition

Expressing past
experience

Before and *after*: −기 전에 and
−ㄴ/은 후에

토요일에 같이 영화를 보러 가는게 어때요?

Why don't we go to see a movie together on Saturday?

아, 좋아요. 뭘 볼까요?

That's good. What shall we see?

이 영화는 어때요?

What about this movie?

네, 그럼 그걸로 봐요!

Yes, then let's see that!

점심을 같이 먹는게 어때요?

Why don't we eat lunch together?

네, 좋아요. 어디서 먹을까요?

Yes, by all means. Where shall we eat?

회사 앞의 이탈리아 식당이 어때요?

What about the Italian restaurant in front of the company?

네, 그럼 거기로 가요.

Yes. Then, let's go there.

내일 같이 테니스를 치는 게 어때요?

Why don't we play tennis together tomorrow?

네, 좋아요. 어디서 칠까요?

Yes, that would be good. Where shall we play?

역 건너 공원이 어때요?

What about the park across from the station?

네. 그럼 그렇게 해요!

Yes. Let's do so!

✎ Work Out 1

Translate the following sentences into Korean using the words inside the parentheses. You will also need to add the appropriate particles.

1. *Why don't we listen to music together?* (듣는 게, 같이, 어때요, 음악)

_____

2. *What kind of music shall we listen to?* (음악, 어떤, 들을까요)

_____

3. *Let's listen to Korean music!* (음악, 들어요, 한국)

_____

4. *Why don't we talk at a café?* (카페, 어때요, 이야기하는 게)

_____

5. *Which café shall we go to?* (갈까요, 어떤, 카페)

_____

6. *Let's go to the café that is next to the university.* (옆에, 카페, 대학, 가요)

_____

7. *When shall we make it?* (언제, 할까요?)

_____

8. *Let's make bibimbop on Sunday!* (일요일, 만들어요 , 비빔밥)

_____

9. *Why don't we buy a new TV?* (어때요, 새, 텔레비전, 사는 게)

_____

10. *Where shall we buy it?* (살까요, 어디서)

_____

11. *Let's buy a TV at the department store!* (텔레비전, 사요, 백화점)

_____

ANSWER KEY
1. 같이 음악(을) 듣는 게 어때요? 2. 어떤 음악(을)들을까요? 3. 한국 음악(을) 들어요! 4. 카페에서 이야기하는 게 어때요? 5. 어떤 카페에 갈까요? 6. 대학 옆에 카페로 가요. 대학 옆에 있는 카페에 가요. 7. 언제 할까요? 8. 일요일에 비빔밥을 만들어요! 9. 새 텔레비전을 사는 게 어때요? 10. 어디서 살까요? 11. 백화점에서 텔레비전을 사요!

🔊 Conversation 2
▶ 8C Conversation 2

Jeongmin has brought her business partner Mr. Smith to a seafood restaurant in Seoul. They have just finished their meal.

정민:	생선 요리가 어떠셨어요?
스미스:	정말 맛있었습니다.
정민:	좋네요. 이 레스토랑에 한번 와 보고 싶었는데 기회가 없었어요.
스미스:	그렇군요. 그 오징어 요리는 어땠어요?
정민:	이 오징어 요리도 좋았어요. 다른 재료들하고 새우, 오징어 그리고 홍합도 요리에 있었는데 아주 양이 많았지만 다 먹었네요.
스미스:	저도 같이 먹었으니까요 ...
정민:	와인 좀 더 안 하시겠어요?
스미스:	사실 어제 술을 좀 너무 많이 마셨어요. 정 이사님을 뵈었을 때 맥주 상품권을 주셨는데 호텔 근처에서 맥주 열 병을 사서 다 마시게 됐어요.
정민:	그렇군요. 그럼 디저트하고 커피나 그런 거를 주문하는게 어때요?
스미스:	네, 찬 디저트를 먹고 싶네요.

Expressing desires: –고
싶었어요 (past tense)

–면 됩니다 (*will do/would do*)

정민:	글쎄요, 메뉴를 한번 더 보죠. 케익만 있네요.
스미스:	저는 아이스크림을 먹고 싶었는데 ... 그럼 저는 커피면 됩니다.
정민:	저는 초콜릿 케익하고 차로 할게요/할래요.

Jeongmin:	*How was that fish dish?*
Smith:	*It was really delicious.*
Jeongmin:	*That's good. I wanted to come to this restaurant once, but I haven't had a chance (until now).*
Smith:	*I see. How was that squid dish?*
Jeongmin:	*The squid dish was also good. Shrimp, squid and mussels were also in the dish, among other ingredients; and it was a very big dish, but I finished eating it all.*
Smith:	*But, I also had a little bit of your dish, so ...*
Jeongmin:	*Wouldn't you like to have a little more wine?*
Smith:	*Actually, I had a little too much to drink yesterday. When I saw Regional Manager Jeong, he gave me a beer gift certificate, so I bought ten bottles of beer near the hotel and ended up drinking everything.*
Jeongmin:	*I see. Then, why don't we order dessert and coffee or something like that?*
Smith:	*Yes, I'd like (lit: to eat) a cold dessert.*
Jeongmin:	*Well, let's take a look at the menu again. There are only cakes.*
Smith:	*Well, I wanted to eat ice cream but ... I am okay with only coffee then.*
Jeongmin:	*Then, I will have a chocolate cake and tea.*

✎ Conversation Practice 2

Fill in the blanks in the following sentences with the missing words. If you're unsure of the answer, listen to the conversation one more time.

1. 이 레스토랑에 한번 와_____싶었는데 기회가 없었어요.

2. 다른 재료들하고 새우, 오징어 그리고_____요리에 있었는데 아주 양이 많았지만 다 먹었네요.

3. 와인 좀 더_____하시겠어요?

4. 정 이사님을_____때 맥주 상품권을 주셨는데 호텔 근처에서 맥주 열 병을

사서 다 마시게 됐었어요.

5. 그럼 디저트하고 커피나 그런 거를_____어때요?

ANSWER KEY
1. 보고 2. 홍합도 3. 안 4. 뵈었을 5. 주문하는 게

Grammar Builder 2

▶ 8D Grammar Builder 2

–면 됩니다 *(WILL DO/WOULD DO)*

To express the conditional *will do/would do*, use –면 됩니다. If the word ends with a consonant, you will need to use a dummy vowel 이 in front of 면.

뭐 주문하시겠어요?
What would you like to order?
저는 커피면 됩니다.
Coffee will do for me.

어떤 음식을 좋아하세요?
What kind of food do you like?
저는 생선 요리면 됩니다.
A fish dish will do for me.

디저트하고 커피나 그런 거를 주문할까요?
Shall we order dessert and coffee or something?
저는 단 거면 됩니다.
Sweets would do for me.

빨간색 스웨터를 드릴까요, 파란색 스웨터를 드릴까요?

Shall I give you a red sweater or a blue sweater?

아무 거나 주시면 됩니다.

You can give me anything. (Anything will do for me.)

어떤 사람을 보내드릴까요?

What kind of person should I send you?

학생이면 됩니다.

Any student will do.

음료수 주문하시겠어요?

Would you like to order a drink?

찬 거면 됩니다.

Anything cold will do.

✎ Work Out 2

Answer the following questions with the word given in the parentheses. Don't forget to alternate between 이면 and 면 depending on how it ends in the preceding noun.

1. a: 무슨 음식을 좋아하세요? (한국 음식)

What kind of food do you like?

b: _____ 됩니다.

Any Korean food will do.

2. a: 빨간색으로 드릴까요, 하얀색으로 드릴까요? (하얀색)

Shall I give you this in red or white?

Expressing past experience

Before and *after*: –기 전에 and –ㄴ/은 후에

b: _____됩니다.

White will do for me.

3. a: 디저트나 커피를 드실래요? (아이스크림)

Would you like dessert or coffee?

b: _____됩니다.

Ice cream will do for me.

4. a: 어떤 색을 좋아하세요? (밝은색)

Which color do you like?

b: _____됩니다.

A bright color will do.

5. a: 미국 음식을 좋아하세요? (햄버거)

Do you like American food?

b: 네, 점심에는_____됩니다.

Yes, at lunch, a hamburger will do for me.

ANSWER KEY
1. 한국 음식이면 2. 하얀색이면 3. 아이스크림이면 4. 밝은 색이면 5. 햄버거면

✎ Drive It Home

Fill in the blanks with the appropriate words to complete the following sentences.

1. 테니스를 치는게_____?

Why don't we play tennis?

2. 테니스를_____?

Shall we play tennis?

3. 테니스를_____!

   Let's play tennis !

4. 음악을 듣는 게_____?

   Why don't we listen to music?

5. 음악을 _____?

   Shall we listen to music?

6. 음악을_____!

   Let's listen to music !

7. 커피면 _____.

   Coffee will do.

8. _____됩니다.

   Any student will do.

9. _____됩니다.

   Ten people would do.

10. _____됩니다.

    White (color) will do.

ANSWER KEY

1. 어때요 2. 칠까요 3. 쳐요 4. 어때요 5. 들을까요 6. 들어요 7. 됩니다 8. 학생이면 9. 열 명이면 10. 하얀색이면

How Did You Do?

Let's see how you did! By now, you should be able to:

☐ express *Let's … , Why don't we … ?, Shall we … ?* (Still unsure? Jump back to Grammar Builder 1.)

☐ express *will do/would do*. (Still unsure? Jump back to Grammar Builder 2.)

Don't forget to practice and reinforce what you've learned by visiting **www.livinglanguage.com/languagelab** for flashcards, games, and quizzes!

✎ Word Recall

1. 블라우스	a. *pink*
2. 노란색	b. *red*
3. 초록색	c. *yellow*
4. 바지	d. *blouse*
5. 파란색	e. *green*
6. 분홍색	f. *pants*
7. 회색	g. *blue*
8. 스웨터	h. *sweater*
9. 갈색	i. *gray*
10. 빨간색	j. *brown*

ANSWER KEY
1. d; 2. c; 3. e; 4. f; 5. g; 6. a; 7. i; 8. h; 9. j; 10. b

Unit 2 Quiz

Let's put the most essential Korean words and grammar points you've learned so far to practice in a few exercises. It's important to be sure that you've mastered this material before you move on. Score yourself at the end of the unit quiz and see if you need to go back for more practice, or if you're ready to move on to Unit 3.

A. Fill in the blanks with the appropriate giving and receiving verbs listed below. Change them into their appropriate forms as necessary.
드리세요, 줬어요, 드릴 거예요, 받았어요, 보세요

1. 학생들에게 한국어를 가르쳐_____.

   I taught Korean to students.

2. 선생님께 빨리 가_____.

   Please go to the teacher quickly.

3. 할머니께 이 우산을 갖다_____.

   Please give this umbrella to grandmother.

4. 큰 아버지 생신에 온 가족이 큰 선물을_____.

   All the family members will give a big gift to an older brother of the father on his birthday.

5. 부모님에게서 비싼 카메라를_____.

   I received an expensive camera from my parents.

B. Based on the English translation, fill in the blanks to express something that you experienced before.

1. 맥주를 다섯 병 마신_____ 있어요.

   I have drunk five bottles of beer.

2. 사장님과 일해_____적이 있어요?

   Have you worked with our company's president?

3. 스파게티를 _____ 본 적이 있어요?

   Have you ever tried making spaghetti?

C. Change the following phrases into the –ㅆ/었/았던 form.

1. 열 사람한테는_____음식

   the food that was insufficient for ten people

2. _____영화

   the movie that was interesting/funny

3. 아주_____한국 음식

   the Korean food that was very spicy

D. Fill in the blanks by modifying the verb in the parentheses with either –기 전에 **or** –ㄴ/은 후에.

1. 저녁_____숙제를 했어요. *(먹다)*

   I did my homework before eating dinner.

2. _____점심을 먹었어요. *(미팅하다)*

   After having the meeting, I ate lunch.

3. 영화를_____표를 샀어요. *(보다)*

   We bought tickets before watching the movie.

E. Write the matching honorific nouns from the word bank.
   댁, 진지, 연세

1. 집: ____

2. 나이: _____

3. 밥: _____

F. Read the following short dialogue and fill in the blanks with appropriate forms.

1. 부장님, 자제분들이_____?

   Do you have children, Division Manager?

2. ____이 두 명 있어요.

   I have two daughters.

3. 사장님께서 녹차를 좋아하시니까 많이_____.

   The president likes green tea, so I think he/she'll drink a lot.

How Did You Do?

Give yourself a point for every correct answer, then use the following key to tell whether you're ready to move on:

0–7 points: It's probably a good idea to go back through the lesson again. You may be moving too quickly, or there may be too much "down time" between your contact with Korean. Remember that it's better to spend 30 minutes with Korean three or four times a week than it is to spend two or three hours just once a week. Find a pace that's comfortable for you, and spread your contact hours out as much as you can.

8-12 points: You would benefit from a review before moving on. Go back and spend a little more time on the specific points that gave you trouble. Re-read the Grammar Builder sections that were difficult, and do the Work Outs one more time. Don't forget about the online supplemental practice material, either. Go to **www.livinglanguage.com/languagelab** for games and quizzes that will reinforce the material from this unit.

13-17 points: Good job! There are just a few points that you could consider reviewing before moving on. If you haven't worked with the games and quizzes on **www.livinglanguage.com/languagelab**, please give them a try.

18-20 points: Great! You're ready to move on to the next unit.

points

Unit 3:
Sports and Hobbies

In Unit 3, you will learn how to talk about your favorite sports and hobbies. Also, some key expressions for asking other people questions about their favorite sports and hobbies will be introduced. By the end of the unit, you'll be able to talk about sports and hobbies and talk further about past experiences. You'll be able to express wants (*to want X*) and abilities (*I can, I'm able to*), and compare items to each other (*X is more than Y; X is the most*). You'll learn how to use relative clauses in Korean, as well as create nouns out of verbs and express *something, someone, somewhere* and *nothing, nobody*, and *nowhere*. Ready to get started?

Lesson 9: Words

In this lesson you'll learn how to:

☐ use key vocabulary related to sports and hobbies.

☐ express *something, someone, somewhere*, and *nothing, nobody*, and *nowhere*.

☐ create nouns out of verbs.

Word Builder 1
▷ 9A Word Builder 1

운동	exercise(s), sports
축구	soccer

배구	volleyball
수영	swimming
유도	judo
검도	kendo
태권도	taekwondo
테니스 코트	tennis court
클럽	club
경기	game (sports)
다음 번	next time
뛰어난	excellent
실력	skill
실력이 안 좋은	unskillful
잘하다	to be good at
잘 못하다	to be bad at
운동하다	to exercise
수영하다	to swim
레슨받다	to take lessons on
하다	to do

✎ Word Practice 1

Translate the following words or phrases into Korean.

exercise(s), sports	1.
swimming	2.
game (sports)	3.
next time	4.
excellent	5.
unskillful	6.

to be good at	7.
to be bad at	8.
to exercise	9.

ANSWER KEY
1. 운동 2. 수영 3. 경기 4. 다음 번 5. 뛰어난 6. 실력이 안 좋은 7. 잘하다 8. 잘 못하다 9. 운동하다

Grammar Builder 1

▶ 9B Grammar Builder 1

INDEFINITE PRONOUNS

Let's learn the indefinite pronouns in Korean: *something/anything, someone/anyone,* and *somewhere/anywhere.*

Indefinite pronouns are used when the speaker has no specific referent in mind. In Korean, question words and indefinite pronouns have the same forms but they differ in intonation.

	QUESTION WORD	INDEFINITE PRONOUN
누구/누가	*who*	*someone/anyone*
뭐(무엇)	*what*	*something/anything*
어디	*where*	*somewhere/anywhere*
언제	*when*	*sometime/anytime*

Let's look at 어디 as an example.

어제 어디 갔어요?
Where did you go yesterday?
학교에 갔어요.
I went to school.

어제 어디 갔어요?
Did you go somewhere/anywhere yesterday?

학교에 갔어요./네, 어디 갔어요.

I went to school./Yes, I went somewhere.

In the first example, 어디 is used as a question word; in the second, as an indefinite pronoun. Let's look at a few more examples of indefinite pronouns.

오늘 누구 만나요?

Are you meeting someone today?

제 한국어 책이 없네요.

It seems that I don't have my Korean book.
방 안 어디에 있을 거예요.

It should be somewhere in the room.

어디 맛있는 식당으로 가고 싶어요.

I want to go to a delicious restaurant somewhere.
그럼 명동으로 갈까요?

Then shall we go to Myeong-Dong?

When these words are used in answer to a question, they will become *anything/nothing, anyone/no one, anywhere/nowhere.*

아무것	*anything/nothing*
아무	*anyone/no one*
아무 데	*anywhere/nowhere*

These words will be marked by a particle depending on whether they appear in a positive sentence that gives an option or in a negative sentence. For positive sentences that give an option, these words will be followed by the particle –(이)나.

뭐 드릴까요?

What should I give you?

아무것이나 주세요.

Give me anything.

–이나 is attached to 아무 in the above sentence to mark "option." *Give me anything* means one or the other is fine, therefore it means there is an option. Let's look at more examples with options:

파티에 누구를 데리고 올까요?

Whom should I bring to the party?

아무나 친한 친구를 데리고 오세요.

Bring anyone close to you.

어디로 드라이브를 갈까요?

Where should we go for a drive?

아무데나 괜찮습니다.

Anywhere is fine.

When you give an option, use –나 after 아무.

In negative sentences, you will mark the grammatical relationship with the particle –도 following the indefinite pronoun.

운동 실력이 좋으세요?

Do you have any sports skills?

아무것도 잘 못해요.

No, I don't do any (of them) well.

축구할 사람들이 어디 있어요?

Where are the people who will play soccer?

아무도 보이지 않네요.

I can't see anyone.

Creating nouns from verbs:
nominalizer –기 or –ㅁ/음

Expressing desire with –(으)면
좋겠어요 (*I wish* …)

어제 누구를 만났어요?

Did you meet someone yesterday?

아니요, 아무도 안 만났어요.

No, I did not meet anyone.

아이가 어디로 갔어요?

Where did the kid go?

아무 데도 없는데요.

The kid is nowhere.

아무것 and 아무데 are derived from the 아무 + noun form. So if it's easier,
remember the following formula when using indefinite pronouns: 아무 + noun +
(이)나/도. Again, to review:

Positive sentences giving an option	아무것/아무/아무데/아무 noun + –(이)나
Negative sentences	아무것/아무/아무데/아무 noun + –도

✎ Work Out 1

Fill in the blanks with the appropriate expressions to complete the sentences.

1. _____영화나 보고 싶어요?

   Do you want to see any movies?

2. _____보고싶지 않아요.

   I don't want to see any.

3. 어제_____갔어요?

   Did you go anywhere yesterday?

4. 아니요, _____ 안 갔어요.

No, I didn't go anywhere.

5. 내일 _____ 볼 거예요?

Will you see anyone tomorrow?

6. 아니요, _____ 안 볼 거예요.

No, I won't see anyone.

ANSWER KEY
1. 아무 2. 아무것도 3. 어디 4. 아무 데도 5. 누구를 6. 아무도

Word Builder 2
▶ 9C Word Builder 2

취미	*hobby*
특기	*special ability, special skill*
그림 그리기	*painting, drawing*
책 읽기	*reading books*
영화 감상	*seeing movies (lit: movie appreciation)*
사진	*photograph*
악기	*musical instrument*
피아노	*piano*
바이올린	*violin*
첼로	*cello*
플루트	*flute*
클라리넷	*clarinet*
콘서트	*concert*
가지고 있다	*to own, to hold*
공연하다	*to perform (musical instruments)*

Creating nouns from verbs:
nominalizer –기 or –ㅁ/음

연주하다	*to play (piano)*
불다	*to play (a wind instrument)*
치다	*to play (a percussion instrument, piano, guitar, tennis, golf, etc)*
원하다	*to want*

✎ Word Practice 2

Translate the following words into Korean.

hobby	1.
special ability, special skill	2.
painting, drawing	3.
reading books	4.
seeing movies (lit: movie appreciation)	5.
photography, photograph	6.
musical instrument	7.
concert	8.
to own, to hold	9.
to perform (musical instruments)	10.

ANSWER KEY
1. 취미 2. 특기 3. 그림 그리기 4. 책 읽기 5. 영화 감상 6. 사진 7. 악기 8. 콘서트 9. 가지고 있다
10. 연주하다

Grammar Builder 2

▶ 9D Grammar Builder 2

CREATING NOUNS FROM VERBS: NOMINALIZER –기 OR –ㅁ/음

As mentioned in the previous lesson, you can create nouns out of verbs in Korean
by adding the nominalizers –기 or –ㅁ/음 to them. These Korean nouns usually

correspond to English nouns ending in –*ing*; e.g. *writing, knitting*. –기 and –ㅁ/음 follow the plain form of verbs.

자다 + 기 = 자기 (*sleeping*)

자다 + ㅁ = 잠 (*sleeping*)

먹다 + 기 = 먹기 (*eating*)

먹다 + 음 = 먹음 (*eating*)

In the –ㅁ/음 form, use –음 after a consonant ending and use –ㅁ after a vowel ending.

In most cases –기 and –ㅁ/음 are interchangeable, but there are also some differences between the two. –기 is often involved in various grammar patterns such as –기가 나쁘다 *it is bad in … ing* or –기가 좋다 *it is good in … ing*. –기 is a more colloquial normalizer, while –ㅁ/음 is used more often in written forms and public signs such as 수심이 깊음 ("*deep water*") or 이곳부터는 더 갈 수 없음 ("*no passing beyond this point*").

저는 먹기와 자기를 좋아해요.
I like eating and sleeping.

밤늦게 일하기는 안 좋아해요.
I don't like working late at night.

피아노 치기를 잘해요.
I'm good at playing the piano.

한국말 하기는 쉬워요.
Speaking Korean is easy.

Creating nouns from verbs:
nominalizer –기 or –ㅁ/음

그림 그리기는 잘 못해요.
I'm bad at painting pictures.

책 읽기는 재미있어요.
Reading books is fun.

제 취미는 요리하기예요.
My hobby is cooking.

제 취미는 영화 보기입니다.
My hobby is watching movies.

김여진 씨께 이 상을 수여함.
Giving this award to Ms. Kim Yeo-Jin.

날씨 맑음.
It's fine weather. (lit: Being fine weather.)

흐림.
It's cloudy. (lit: Being cloudy.)

이 구역에서는 흡연을 금지함.
No smoking in this area.

✎ Work Out 2

Translate the following Korean sentences into English.

1. 중국어 쓰기는 어려워요.

2. 제 취미는 바이올린 연주하기입니다.

_____

3. 친구들과 같이 나가기는 재미있습니다.

_____

4. 영화보기를 좋아합니다.

_____

5. 제 특기는 플루트 불기입니다.

_____

6. 7시에 같이 학교를 감.

_____

7. 축구를 못함.

_____

ANSWER KEY
1. *Writing Chinese is difficult.* 2. *My hobby is playing the violin.* 3. *Going out with friends is enjoyable/fun.* 4. *I like watching movies.* 5. *My special skill is playing the flute.* 6. *Going to school together at 7.* 7. *Poor at playing soccer.*

✎ Drive It Home

A. Fill in the blanks with appropriate particles.

1. 특별한 취미_____있어요?

Do you have any special skills?

2. 어제 누_____왔어요?

Did anyone come yesterday?

3. 아무_____안 왔어요.

   No one came.

4. 주말에 어디____ 갔어요?

   Did you go anywhere on the weekend?

5. 아무 데_____안 갔어요.

   I didn't go anywhere.

B. Fill in the blanks with appropriate words.

1. 저는_____와 _____를 좋아합니다.

   I like eating and sleeping.

2. 공부하____는 별로 안 좋아합니다.

   I don't like studying so much.

3. 피아노 _____를 잘해요.

   I'm good at playing the piano.

4. 한국말_____는 쉬워요.

   Speaking Korean is easy.

ANSWER KEY
A. 1. 가 2. 가 3. 도 4. 에 5. 도
B. 1. 먹기, 자기 2. 기 3. 치기 4. 하기

🌐 Culture Note

Sports are extremely popular in Korea. While soccer (축구) is certainly the most
popular sport, especially after Korea and Japan hosted the 2002 World Cup
Championships, Koreans enjoy other pastimes as well. The national martial
art is 태권도 (*taekwondo*) which is still a popular sport exercised throughout
the nation. Nowadays, Koreans also enjoy baseball and basketball, and have

professional leagues for both sports. Some Korean players are recruited to the MLB or NBA in the United States. If you ever have the chance to attend a sporting match in Korea, you can keep these two chants in mind: 대/한/민국! (lit: *Great-Korean-nation!*) and 이겨라! (*Victory!*). You'll probably hear them a lot, as Koreans are huge sports fans and big supporters of their national teams.

How Did You Do?

Let's see how you did! By now, you should be able to:

☐ use key vocabulary related to sports and hobbies. (Still unsure? Jump back to Word Builder 1 or Word Builder 2.)

☐ express *something, someone, somewhere,* and *nothing, nobody,* and *nowhere.* (Still unsure? Jump back to Grammar Builder 1.)

☐ create nouns out of verbs. (Still unsure? Jump back to Grammar Builder 2.)

✎ Word Recall

1. 모	a. *necktie*
2. 무거운	b. *solid (color)*
3. 넥타이	c. *dark*
4. 면	d. *heavy*
5. 정가	e. *wool*
6. 단색의	f. *exchange*
7. 어두운	g. *cotton*
8. 사이즈	h. *jeans*
9. 청바지	i. *price*
10. 교환하다	j. *size*

ANSWER KEY
1. e; 2. d; 3. a; 4. g; 5. i; 6. b; 7. c; 8. j; 9. h; 10. f

Lesson 10: Phrases

In this lesson you'll learn how to:

☐ express *can do* and *be able to do*.

☐ express your desire with –(으)면 좋겠어요.

Phrase Builder 1

▷ 10A Phrase Builder 1

어떤 운동	*what kind of sports*
태권도 클럽	*taekwondo club*
야구와 축구	*baseball and soccer*
유도나 검도	*judo or kendo*
학생이었을 때	*when I was a student*
경기가 있으면	*if/when there's a game*
집 근처 테니스 코트	*tennis court near my house*
주말에 사용하는 테니스 코트	*the tennis court I'm using on weekends*
두 시간 쯤	*for about two hours*
특히	*especially*
몇 번	*several times*
테니스를 잘 치다	*to be good at tennis*
테니스를 잘 못 치다	*to be bad at tennis*
수학을 잘하다	*to be good at mathematics*
수학을 못하다	*to be poor at mathematics*
야구를 하다	*to play baseball*
클럽에 있다	*to be in a club*
운동을 하다	*to play some sports; to exercise*

운동을 안 하다	*to play no sports; to not exercise*
아무 운동을 안 하다	*to not play any sports; to not do any exercise*
그저 그래요	*So-so.*

✎ Phrase Practice 1

Fill in the missing words below.

1. 유도_____검도

   judo or kendo

2. 두_____쯤

   for about two hours

3. 몇_____

   several times

4. 테니스를 잘_____

   be good at tennis

5. 테니스를 잘_____치다

   be bad at tennis

6. 수학_____잘하다

   be good at mathematics

7. 수학을_____하다

   be poor at mathematics

   ANSWER KEY
   1. 나 2. 시간 3. 번 4. 치다 5. 못 6. 을 7. 못

Grammar Builder 1

▷ 10B Grammar Builder 1

CAN DO AND *BE ABLE TO DO*

We learned that potential forms of verbs can be used to express the meaning of
the English *can/to be able to* + verb earlier in *Intermediate Korean*. Let's review
them by using various verbs in their potential forms to express more diverse
sentences. Don't forget to put a space before and after 수.

VERB + –ㄹ/–을 수 있다 = *CAN*			
가다	갈 수 있다 *can go*	자다	잘 수 있다 *can sleep*
오다	올 수 있다 *can come*	공부하다	공부할 수 있다 *can study*
치다	칠 수 있다 *can hit/play*	말하다	말할 수 있다 *can speak*
하다	할 수 있다 *can do*	여행하다	여행할 수 있다 *can travel*
먹다	먹을 수 있다 *can eat*	연주하다	연주할 수 있다 *can play musical instrument*
보다	볼 수 있다 *can see*	잘하다	잘할 수 있다 *can do well*
듣다	들을 수 있다 *can hear*	수영하다	수영할 수 있다 *can swim*

Now let's take a look at some negative potential forms, meaning *cannot*.

VERB + ㄹ/을 수 없다 = *CANNOT*			
가다	갈 수 없다 *cannot go*	자다	잘 수 없다 *cannot sleep*

VERB + ㄹ/을 수 없다 = *CANNOT*			
오다	올 수 없다 *cannot come*	공부하다	공부할 수 없다 *cannot study*
치다	칠 수 없다 *cannot hit/play*	말하다	말할 수 없다 *cannot speak*
하다	할 수 없다 *cannot do*	여행하다	여행할 수 없다 *cannot travel*

The potential forms also have tenses. Let's take a look at the past potential forms.

VERB + ㄹ/을 수 있었다 = *COULD*			
가다	갈 수 있었다 *could go*	자다	잘 수 있었다 *could sleep*
오다	올 수 있었다 *could come*	공부하다	공부할 수 있었다 *could study*

VERB + ㄹ/을 수 없었다 = *COULD NOT*			
치다	칠 수 없었다 *could not hit/play*	말하다	말할 수 없었다 *could not speak*
하다	할 수 없었다 *could not do*	여행하다	여행할 수 없었다 *could not travel*

Now the future forms.

VERB + ㄹ/을 수 있을 거예요 = *WILL BE ABLE TO*			
가다	갈 수 있을 거예요 *will be able to go*	자다	잘 수 있을 거예요 *will be able to sleep*
오다	올 수 있을 거예요 *will be able to come*	공부하다	공부할 수 있을 거예요 *will be able to study*

VERB + ㄹ/을 수 없을 거예요 = *WILL NOT BE ABLE TO*			
치다	칠 수 없을 거예요 *will not be able to hit/play*	말하다	말할 수 없을 거예요 *will not be able to speak*
하다	할 수 없을 거예요 *will not be able to do*	여행하다	여행할 수 없을 거예요 *will not be able to travel*

태권도를 할 수 있어요?

Can you do taekwondo?

네, 조금 할 수 있어요./아니요, 전혀 못해요.

Yes, I can do a little./No, I cannot do it at all.

내일 아침 다섯 시에 일어날 수 있어요?

Can you get up at 5:00 a.m. tomorrow?

일어날 수 있어요./일어날 수 없어요.

I can get up./I can't get up.

매운 음식을 먹을 수 있어요?

Can you eat spicy food?

아니요, 너무 매운 음식은 먹을 수 없어요.

No, I cannot eat food that's too spicy.

어떤 말을 할 수 있어요?

What languages can you speak?

영어와 스페인어를 할 수 있어요.

I can speak English and Spanish.

수학 숙제를 할 수 있었어요?

Were you able to do the mathematics homework?

네, 할 수 있었어요./아니요, 너무 어려워서 할 수 없었어요.
Yes, I was able to do it./No, it was too difficult, so I couldn't do it.

일요일에 도서관에 올 수 있어요?
Can you come to the library on Sunday?
네, 갈 수 있어요./아니요, 갈 수 없어요.
Yes, I can come./No, I can't come.

한국말 할 수 있어요?
Can you speak Korean?
네, 여름까지는 한국말을 할 수 있을 거예요.
Yes, I will be able to speak Korean by the summer.

✎ Work Out 1

A. Complete the sentences using the appropriate form in the blanks, based on the English translations.

1. 파티에_____수 있어요?

   Can you go to the party?

2. 진섭 씨와 이야기할_____없었어요.

   I couldn't talk with Mr. Jin-Seop.

3. 내일 학교에 갈 수_____.

   I cannot go to school tomorrow.

4. 미팅에_____수 있어요?

   Can you attend the meeting?

5. 유명한 그림을_____수 없었어요.

I couldn't see the famous painting.

6. 운동을_____수 있어요?

Can you play any sports?

B. Translate the following Korean sentences into English.

1. 언니는 피아노를 치고 바이올린을 연주할 수 있어요.

_____

2. 우리 아버지께서는 요리를 할 수 없으세요/할 수 없어요.

_____

3. 오늘 선생님을 볼 수 없었습니다.

_____

4. 어제 세미나에 참석할 수 없었습니다.

_____

5. 이건 중요한 것이니까 아무에게도 줄 수 없습니다.

_____

ANSWER KEY
A. 1. 갈 2. 수 3. 없어요 4. 참석할 5. 볼 6. 할
B. 1. *My older sister can play the piano and the violin.* 2. *My father cannot cook.* 3. *I couldn't see my teacher today.* 4. *I couldn't attend the seminar yesterday.* 5. *This is an important thing, so I cannot give it to anyone.*

Phrase Builder 2
▶ 10C Phrase Builder 2

| 바이올린, 첼로 그리고 피아노 | *the violin, the cello and the piano* |

종로의 레스토랑	a restaurant in Jongro
다음 토요일	next Saturday
그림 그리기와 책 읽기	painting and reading books
사진 찍기	taking photos
닉슨 씨가 그린 그림	the painting that Ms. Nixon painted
지금 사용하는 바이올린	the violin I am using now
새 거	new one
새 거를 샀으면 좋겠어요	I would like a new one
사실은	actually
지금까지	up to now
콘서트에서	at a concert
일주일에 두 권쯤	about two books a week
악기를 좀 연주할 수 있어요	I can play musical instruments a little
악기는 연주할 수 없어요	I can play no musical instruments
. . . 레슨을 받다	to take lessons on . . .
카메라를 가지고 나가다	to go out with a camera
대단하네요!	That's amazing!

✎ Phrase Practice 2

Complete the following by inserting appropriate words.

1. 바이올린, _____그리고 피아노

   the violin, the cello and the piano

2. 종로____레스토랑

   a restaurant in Jongro

3. _____토요일

next Saturday

4. 사진_____

taking photos

5. 닉슨 씨____그린 그림

the painting that Ms. Nixon painted

6. 새____

new one

7. 지금_____

up to now

8. 콘서트_____

at a concert

ANSWER KEY
1. 첼로 2. 의 3. 다음 4. 찍기 5. 가 6. 거 7. 까지 8. 에서

Grammar Builder 2
▶ 10D Grammar Builder 2

EXPRESSING DESIRE WITH –(으)면 좋겠어요 (*I WISH …*)

You learned how to express a desire to do something in *Intermediate Korean* using
the grammar pattern –고 싶다, as in 한국말을 배우고 싶어요 (*I want to learn
Korean.*) There are other grammar patterns you can use to express desire; one of
them is –(으)면 좋겠어요. This expression would directly translate into English
something like: *If it is …, I would like it.* You will use –으면 좋겠어요 after words
ending in a consonant and –면 좋겠어요 after words ending in a vowel.

집이 크면 좋겠어요.
I wish the house were big./I hope the house is big.

케익이 맛있으면 좋겠어요.
I wish the cake were delicious.

제가 테니스 경기를 잘 하면 좋겠어요.
I wish I played tennis (games) well.

피아노를 잘 연주하면 좋겠어요.
I wish I played the piano well.

한국말을 더 잘 하면 좋겠어요.
I wish I spoke Korean better.

✎ Work Out 2

Translate the following Korean sentences into English.

1. 새 컴퓨터를 가지고 싶지만 비싸서 살 수 없어요.

   _____

2. 한국말을 배우고 있으니까 한국말을 더 잘 하고 싶어요.

   _____

3. 한국에 가서 태권도를 배우고 싶어요.

   _____

4. 더 큰 방이 있으면 좋겠어요.

   _____

5. 남동생이 좋은 대학에 가면 좋겠어요.

ANSWER KEY

1. *I want a new computer, but I cannot buy one because it's expensive. 2. Because I am learning Korean I want to speak Korean better. 3. I want to go to Korea and learn taekwondo. 4. I wish I had a bigger room. 5. I wish my younger brother went to a good college.*

✎ Drive It Home

A. Fill in the blanks by choosing appropriate words from the word bank.

할, 읽을, 일어날

1. 한국 책을_____수 있어요.

   I can read Korean books.

2. 아침 다섯 시에_____수 있어요.

   I can get up at 5 a.m.

3. 영어와 스페인어를_____수 있어요.

   I can speak English and Spanish.

B. Fill in the blanks with appropriate words.

1. 한국 책을 읽을 수_____.

   I can read Korean books.

2. 아침 다섯 시에 일어날 수_____.

   I can get up at 5 a.m.

3. 영어와 스페인어를 할_____있어요.

   I can speak English and Spanish.

C. Fill in the blanks with the appropriate words. Follow the English cues.

1. 새 차가_____좋겠어요.

   I wish I had a new car.

2. 한국말을 잘_____좋겠어요.

   I wish I spoke Korean well.

3. 테니스를 잘_____좋겠어요.

   I wish I could play tennis well.

   ANSWER KEY
   A. 1. 읽을 2. 일어날 3. 할
   B. 1. 있어요 2. 있어요 3. 수
   C. 1. 있으면 2. 하면 3. 치면

💡 Tip!

List five things you can do and five things you cannot do in English. Then say them in Korean using –ㄹ/을 수 있어요. If you don't know the words you need, look them up in an English-Korean dictionary. Having a bilingual dictionary handy as you go through the lessons is an excellent idea (or simply keep the glossary that appears in these course books near at hand). You can look up words whenever you think of them; if you do this regularly, you will considerably expand your vocabulary—a key to communication.

How Did You Do?

Let's see how you did! By now, you should be able to:

☐ express *can do* and *be able to do*. (Still unsure? Jump back to Grammar Builder 1.)

☐ express desire with –(으)면 좋겠어요. (Still unsure? Jump back to Grammar Builder 2.)

✎ Word Recall

1. 양파
2. 양배추
3. 두 분
4. 주스
5. 있어요
6. 된장찌개
7. 감자
8. 음식
9. 찬
10. 추운

a. *two people (honorific)*
b. *juice*
c. *cold (object)*
d. *food*
e. *onion*
f. *cabbage*
g. *there is, to have, to exist (polite)*
h. *bean paste stew*
i. *cold (weather)*
j. *potato*

ANSWER KEY
1. e; 2. f; 3. a; 4. b; 5. g; 6. h; 7. j; 8. d; 9. c; 10. i

Lesson 11: Sentences

In this lesson you'll learn how to:

☐ compare two items using *A is more X than B.*

☐ compare three or more items using *A is the most X among D.*

Sentence Builder 1

▶ 11A Sentence Builder 1

| 어떤 스포츠를 좋아하세요? | *What kind of sports do you like?* |
| 어떤 운동을 하세요? | *What kind of sports do you play?* |

학생이었을 때 농구를 했어요.	When I was a student, I played basketball.
학생이었을 때 태권도를 했었어요.	When I was a student, I used to do taekwondo.
특별히 하는 운동은 없어요.	I am not playing any sport in particular.
테니스 안 치세요?	Don't you play tennis?
종종 집 근처 테니스 코트에 가서 두 시간 쯤 테니스를 쳐요.	I often go to the tennis court near my house and play tennis for about two hours.
테니스 잘 치시지요 ?	You are good at tennis, aren't you?
테니스는 몇 번 쳐 봤는데, 잘 못 쳐요.	I have tried playing tennis several times, but I'm not good at it.
야구하고 축구 보는 것을 아주 좋아해요.	I like watching baseball and soccer very much.
경기가 있으면 늘 텔레비전으로 봐요.	When there is a game, I always watch it on TV.
야구와 축구 중 뭐를 더 좋아하세요?	Which do you like better, baseball or soccer?
야구를 더 좋아해요.	I like baseball better.
태권도나 유도 레슨을 받고 싶지만 지금은 시간이 없어서 . . .	I want to take taekwondo or judo lessons, but I don't have time now, so . . .
레슨을 받는다면 태권도가 검도 보다 더 나은 것 같아요.	If you take lessons, I think taekwondo is better than kendo.
언제 같이 테니스 치지 않으실래요?	Why don't we play tennis together sometime?
저도 잘 못 치니까 괜찮습니다.	I cannot play it well either, so it's okay.
제가 주중에 사용하는 테니스 코트가 사무실 근처에 있어요.	There's a tennis court near the office that I'm using on weekdays.

Creating nouns from verbs: Expressing desire with –(으)면
nominalizer –기 or –ㅁ/음   좋겠어요 (*I wish …*)

| 시간이 있으면 다음에 거기에 가 보지요! | Let's go there next time when we have time! |

✎ Sentence Practice 1

Fill in the missing words in each of the following sentences.

1. 특별히_____운동은 없어요.

   I am not playing any sport in particular.

2. 테니스 잘_____?

   You are good at tennis, aren't you?

3. 야구하고 축구 보는_____아주 좋아해요.

   I like watching baseball and soccer very much.

4. 경기가_____늘 텔레비전으로 봐요.

   When there is a game, I always watch it on TV.

5. 야구와 축구 중 뭐를_____좋아하세요?

   Which do you like better, baseball or soccer?

6. _____더 좋아해요.

   I like baseball better.

7. 태권도나 유도 레슨을 받고_____지금은 시간이 없어서 …

   I want to take taekwondo or judo lessons, but I don't have time now, so …

8. 저도 잘 못_____괜찮습니다.

   I cannot play it well either, so it's okay.

ANSWER KEY
1. 하는 2. 치(시)지요 3. 것을 4. 있으면 5. 더 6. 야구를 7. 싶지만 8. 치니까

Grammar Builder 1

▷ 11B Grammar Builder 1

COMPARATIVES

You can compare two items (A and B, for the purpose of example) using the structure below.

A 이/가 B보다 (더) X	*A is more X than B.*

In this structure, X can be an adjective or a verb. Now, let's look at how this structure can be used in sentences.

미국이 한국보다 더 커요.
The U.S. is bigger than Korea.

이 아파트가 저 아파트보다 더 편리해요.
This apartment is more convenient than that apartment.

불고기가 햄버거보다 더 맛있어요.
Bulgogi is more delicious than hamburgers.

Use 더 많이 in front of the verb to express *more* comparatives.

마이클 씨가 존 씨 보다 더 많이 공부해요.
Mr. Michael studies more than Mr. John.

어제는 오늘보다 더 많이 걸었어요.
I walked yesterday more than I did today.

When asking and answering questions comparing two items, use the following structures.

| A 하고 B 중 뭐가 (더) X? | *Which is more X: A, or B?* |

중 is *among* or *between*. So this structure literally means *between A and B, which one is more … ?* Let's see how these expressions can be used.

커피하고 차 중 뭐가 더 좋으세요?
Which do you like better, coffee or tea?
커피보다 차가 더 좋아요.
I like tea more than coffee.

Remember that –보다 is a particle, so it is attached to the previous word. In other words, there is no space in between the word and the 보다 in this grammatical pattern.

불고기하고 피자 중 뭐가 더 맛있으세요?
Which do you think is more delicious, bulgogi or pizza?
불고기가 더 맛있어요.
I think bulgogi is more delicious.

✎ Work Out 1

A. Translate the following sentences into Korean using the words given in parentheses. Make sure to use the structure A 이/가 B 보다 더 X.

1. *The U.S. is bigger than England.* (미국, 영국, 커요)

_____

2. *This park is quieter than that park.* (이 공원, 저 공원, 조용해요)

_____

3. *This book is more interesting than that book.* (이 책, 저 책, 재미있어요.)

_____

4. *Mr. Jin-Seop exercises more (lit: does more exercises) than Mr. Yong-Min.* (진섭 씨, 용민 씨, 운동하다)

_____

5. *The subway is more convenient than the bus.* (지하철, 버스, 편리해요)

_____

B. Form questions and answers using the words provided in parentheses. Make sure to use the structures A 하고 B 중 뭐가 더 X?

1. (토요일, 일요일, 좋으세요)

   Q. Which do you like better, Saturday or Sunday?

   A. I like Saturday better than Sunday.

_____

2. (녹차, 홍차, 드세요)

   Q. Which do you drink more often, green tea or black tea?

   A. I drink black tea more often.

_____

3. (중국, 일본, 커요)

   Q. Which is bigger, China or Japan?

   A. China is bigger than Japan.

_____

4. (생선 요리, 고기 요리, 맛있어요)

Q. *Which do you think is more delicious, fish-based cuisine or meat-based cuisine?*

A. *I think fish-based cuisine is more delicious.*

5. (맥주, 와인, 좋아하세요)

Q. *Which do you like more, beer or wine?*

A. *I like beer more.*

ANSWER KEY
A. 1. 미국이 영국보다 더 커요. 2. 이 공원이 저 공원보다 더 조용해요. 3. 이 책이 저 책보다 더
재미있어요. 4. 진섭 씨가 용민 씨보다 더 많이 운동을 해요. 5. 지하철이 버스보다 더 편리해요.
B. 1. 토요일하고 일요일 중 뭐가 더 좋으세요? 토요일이 일요일보다 더 좋아요. 2. 녹차하고 홍차 중
뭐를 더 자주 드세요? 홍차를 더 자주 마셔요. 3. 중국하고 일본 중 뭐가 더 커요? 중국이 일본보다
더 커요. 4. 생선 요리하고 고기요리 중뭐가 더 맛있어요? 생선 요리가 더 맛있는 것 같아요.
5. 맥주하고 와인 중 뭐를 더 좋아하세요? 맥주를 더 좋아해요.

Sentence Builder 2

▶ 11C Sentence Builder 2

취미가 있으세요?	*Do you have any hobbies?*
제 취미는 그림 그리기예요.	*My hobby is painting.*
그림 그리기를 좋아해요.	*I like painting.*
사진 찍기를 좋아해요.	*I like taking pictures.*
책 읽기도 좋아해요.	*I like reading books, too.*
일주일에 두 권 쯤 읽어요.	*I read about two books a week.*
로페즈 씨가 그린 그림들을 보고 싶은데요.	*I want to see the paintings that Ms. Lopez painted.*
주말에는 가끔 카메라를 가지고 나가요.	*On the weekend, I often go out and take a camera with me.*

악기를 연주할 수 있으세요?	Can you play any musical instruments?
바이올린, 첼로, 그리고 피아노를 연주할 수 있어요.	I can play the violin, the cello, and the piano.
플루트 레슨을 받고 있는데 잘 연주하지는 못해요.	I am taking flute lessons, but I cannot play it well.
정말 대단하시네요.	It is amazing, isn't it?
바이올린, 첼로, 피아노 중에 어떤 것을 가장 잘 하세요?	Which are you best at, the violin, the cello, or the piano?
20년 동안 레슨을 받았기 때문에 바이올린을 가장 잘 연주해요.	Since I have been taking lessons for twenty years, I am best at the violin.
지금 사용하는 바이올린은 낡아서 새 것을 사고 싶어요.	The violin I am using now is old, so I want to buy a new one.
너무 비싸서 살 수 없어요.	Since it's too expensive, I cannot buy it.
콘서트에서 연주해 본 적이 있어요?	Have you ever performed in a concert?
이번 주 토요일에 대학로 레스토랑에서 연주하는데 오지 않으실래요?	I will perform at a restaurant in Dae Hak Ro this Saturday, so why don't you come?
그럼요!	Sure thing!

✎ Sentence Practice 2

Fill in the missing words in each of the following sentences.

1. 제 취미는 그림_____예요.

   My hobby is painting.

2. 그림 그리기를_____.

   I like painting.

3. 일주일에 두_____쯤 읽어요.

   I read about two books a week.

4. 로페즈 씨가_____그림들을 보고 싶은데요.

   I want to see the paintings that Ms. Lopez painted.

5. 바이올린, 첼로, 피아노_____어떤 것을 가장 잘 하세요?

   Which are you best at, the violin, the cello, or the piano?

6. 너무 비싸서_____수 없어요.

   Since it's too expensive, I cannot buy it.

7. 콘서트에서_____본 적이 있어요?

   Have you ever performed at a concert?

8. 이번 주 토요일에 대학로 레스토랑에서 연주하는데_____않으실래요?

   I will perform at a restaurant in Dae Hak Ro this Saturday, so why don't you come?

   ANSWER KEY
   1. 그리기 2. 좋아해요 3. 권 4. 그린 5. 중에 6. 살 7. 연주해 8. 오지

Grammar Builder 2
▶ 11D Grammar Builder 2

SUPERLATIVES

You can compare three or more items using the structures described below.

A, B, C 중에 A	*A among A, B, and C*
D 중에 A	*Among D, A (where D is a plural category)*
제일/가장 잘 해요	*I do/play the best*

Now, let's see how these structures can be used.

피아노, 바이올린, 플루트 중에 피아노를 제일 잘 해요.
Among the piano, the violin and the flute, I am the best at the piano.

악기 중에 피아노를 제일 잘 연주해요.
Among musical instruments, I'm the best at playing the piano.

마이클, 제임스, 존 씨 중에 제임스 씨가 제일 키가 커요.
Among Mr. Michael, Mr. James, and Mr. John, Mr. James is the tallest.

이 클래스 학생들 중에 영민 씨가 영어를 제일 잘 해요.
Among the students in this class, Ms. Youngmin is the best in English.

음료수 중에 뭐를 제일 좋아하세요?
Among beverages, which do you like best?
오렌지 주스를 제일 좋아해요
I like orange juice best.

주중에 월요일, 화요일, 수요일 중 언제가 제일 바쁘세요?
Which day of the week are you busiest: Monday, Tuesday, or Wednesday?
월요일이 제일 바빠요.
I am busiest on Monday.

✎ Work Out 2

Translate the following sentences into Korean using the expressions given in parentheses. You'll also need to provide the appropriate particles in order to form complete sentences.

1. *Which do you like best: tennis, golf, or jogging?* (중에, 좋아하세요, 테니스, 골프, 조깅, 뭐를)

2. *I am best at the violin among the musical instruments.* (바이올린, 하다, 악기, 제일)

_____

3. *Which country is the biggest: Korea, China, or Japan?* (일본, 중국, 한국, 커요)

_____

4. *Who does play tennis the best among the employees?* (회사원, 테니스, 쳐요)

_____

5. *April is the busiest month of the year (lit: in a year).* (일년, 바쁜, 달)

_____

ANSWER KEY
1. 테니스, 조깅, 골프 중에 뭐를 제일 좋아하세요? 2. 악기 중에 바이올린을 제일 잘 해요. 3. 한국, 중국, 일본 중에 어느 나라가 제일 커요? 4. 회사원 중에 누가테니스를 제일잘 쳐요? 5. 일년 중에 4월이 제일 바쁜 달이에요.

✎ Drive It Home

Fill in the blanks with the appropriate words.

1. 미국하고 영국_____어느 나라가 더 커요?

Which is bigger, the U.S. or England?

2. 미국이 영국_____더 커요.

The U.S. is bigger than England.

3. 이 아파트하고 저 아파트 중에 어느 아파트가_____편리해요?

Which is more convenient, this apartment or that apartment?

4. 이 아파트가 저 아파트보다 더_____.

This apartment is more convenient than that apartment.

5. 녹차, 홍차, 커피_____무엇을 제일 좋아하세요?

Which do you like best: green tea, black tea, or coffee?

6. _____중에 어떤 것을 제일 좋아하세요?

Among beverages, which do you like best?

7. 커피가_____좋아요.

I like coffee best.

ANSWER KEY
1. 중에 2. 보다 3. 더 4. 편리해요 5. 중에 6. 음료수 7. 제일

☀ Tip!

Ask your Korean friends, classmates, or colleagues what their hobbies are in Korean. You can also ask them about their favorite sports and whether or not they have some other special skills, such as painting or playing instruments. You can extend the conversation by asking if there is something they are particularly good at. These topics are easy to talk about, and people will most likely ask you the same questions in return. If there aren't any Korean speakers around you, ask the same questions to your family, friends, or colleagues in English. Write down the information you collect, then try saying it in Korean.

How Did You Do?

Let's see how you did! By now, you should be able to:

☐ compare two items using *A is more X than B*. (Still unsure? Jump back to Grammar Builder 1.)

☐ compare three or more items using *A is the most X among D*. (Still unsure? Jump back to Grammar Builder 2.)

Creating nouns from verbs: Expressing desire with –(으)면
nominalizer –기 or –ㅁ/음   좋겠어요 (*I wish* . . .)

✎ Word Recall

1. 반	a. *amount*
2. 빵	b. *lettuce*
3. 상추	c. *tobacco, cigarette*
4. 밥	d. *half*
5. 양	e. *bread*
6. 오이	f. *cooked rice, meal*
7. 담배	g. *ham*
8. 반찬	h. *dish eaten with cooked rice*
9. 계란	i. *egg*
10. 햄	j. *cucumber*

ANSWER KEY
1. d; 2. e; 3. b; 4. f; 5. a; 6. j; 7. c; 8. h; 9. i; 10. g

Lesson 12: Conversations

In this lesson you'll learn how to:

☐ talk about past experiences.

☐ use relative clauses.

ⒸⒸ Conversation 1

▶ 12A Conversation 1

Mr. Clark and Mr. Min-Joon are talking about sports during a break at work.

민준: 클라크 씨, 어떤 스포츠를 좋아하세요?

클라크: 대학생이었을 때 농구를 했어요. 하지만 지금은 테니스를
        좋아해서 집 근처 테니스 코트에 자주 가고 주말에는 두 시간 쯤
        테니스를 쳐요.

민준: 그럼 테니스 잘 치시겠네요?

클라크: 그저 그래요. 그리고 야구하고 축구 보는 것도 아주 좋아해서
        경기가 있으면 늘 텔레비전으로 봐요.

민준: 그러세요. 야구와 축구 중 뭐를 더 좋아하세요?

클라크: 사실은 야구를 더 좋아해요. 민준 씨는 운동 하세요?

민준: 학생이었을 때 태권도를 한 적이 있었지만 지금은 특별히 하는
        운동은 없어요.

클라크: 그러세요. 태권도는 좋은 운동이지요? 저도 태권도나 검도
        레슨을 받고 싶지만 지금은 시간이 없어서 . . .

민준: 레슨을 받는다면 태권도가 검도보다 더 나은 것 같아요.

클라크: 네, 저도 그렇게 생각해요. 그런데, 민준 씨, 테니스 안 치세요?

민준: 테니스는 몇 번 쳐 봤는데, 잘 못 쳐요.

클라크: 언제 같이 테니스 치지 않으실래요?

민준: 저는 잘 못 쳐서요 . . .

클라크: 저도 잘 못 치니까 괜찮습니다. 제가 주중에 사용하는 테니스
        코트가 사무실 근처에 있는데 거기서 치는게 어때요?

민준: 네, 그럼 시간이 있으면 다음에 거기에 가 보지요!

Min-Joon: *What kinds of sports do you like, Mr. Clark?*

Clark: *I played basketball when I was a college student. But now I like
            tennis, so I go to the tennis court near my house often and play
            tennis for about two hours on weekends.*

Min-Joon: *Well, you are probably good at tennis then, aren't you?*

Clark: *So-so. And, I also like watching baseball and soccer very much, so
            when there is a game, I am always watching it on TV.*

Min-Joon: *I see. And which do you like better, baseball or soccer?*

Clark: *Well, actually I like baseball better. Mr. Min-Joon, do you play any
            sports?*

Min-Joon:	I used to do taekwondo when I was a student, but now I don't play any sport in particular.
Clark:	I see. Taekwondo is a good sport, isn't it? I also want to take taekwondo or kendo lessons, but I don't have time now, so ...
Min-Joon:	If you take lessons, I think taekwondo is better than kendo.
Clark:	Yes. I think so, too. By the way, Mr. Min-Joon, don't you play tennis?
Min-Joon:	I have played several times, but I am not good at it.
Clark:	Why don't we play tennis together sometime?
Ken:	But, I'm not good at it, so ...
Clark:	I cannot play well either, so it's alright. The tennis court that I use on weekdays is near the office, so why don't we play there?
Min-Joon:	Yes, then let's go there when we have time!

✎ Conversation Practice 1

Fill in the blanks in the following sentences. If you're unsure of the answer, listen to the conversation one more time.

1. 지금은 테니스를_____집 근처 테니스 코트에 자주 가고 주말에는 두 시간 쯤 테니스를 쳐요.

2. 야구와 축구 중 뭐를_____좋아하세요?

3. 학생이었을 때 태권도를 한 적이 _____지금은 특별히 하는 운동은 없어요.

4. 레슨을_____태권도가 검도보다 더 나은 것 같아요.

5. 제가 주중에 사용하는 테니스 코트가 사무실 근처에_____거기서 쳐 보는게 어때요?

ANSWER KEY
1. 좋아해서 2. 더 3. 있었지만 4. 받는다면 5. 있는데

Grammar Builder 1

▶ 12B Grammar Builder 1

TALKING ABOUT PAST EXPERIENCES

You can talk about your past experiences using the structure below.

Verb + –어/아 본 적이 있어요 = *I have* + past participle

서울에 가 본 적이 있어요.
I have been to Seoul.

파리에 여행을 해 본 적이 있어요.
I have traveled to Paris.

콘서트에서 연주해 본 적이 있어요.
I have performed in a concert.

When answering a question, you can just use 네, 있어요 (*Yes, I have*) or 아니요, 없어요 (*No, I haven't*) without repeating all the information that was already mentioned in the question.

이 영화를 본 적이 있어요?
Have you seen this movie?
네, 있어요./아니요, 없어요.
Yes, I have./No, I haven't.

The following time expressions are often used with this structure.

한 번	*once*
자주	*many times*
전혀	*never*

아직	not yet
한번도 안 + verb	never once
한번도 + verb 지 않다	

김밥을 만들어 본 적이 있어요?

Have you ever made kim-bob?

네, 한번 만들어 본 적이 있어요.

Yes, I have (made it) once.

중앙 도서관에서 책을 빌려본 적이 있어요?

Have you ever borrowed books from Central Library?

네, 자주요.

Yes, (I have borrowed them) many times.

포르투갈 어를 공부해 본 적이 있어요?

Have you ever studied Portuguese?

아니요, 전혀 없어요.

No, I have never (studied it).

한국어로 리포트를 써 본 적이 있어요?

Have you ever written a report in Korean?

아니요, 아직요.

No, I haven't (written it) yet.

번지 점프를 해 본 적이 있어요?

Have you ever done bungee jumping?

아니요, 한번도 안 해 봤어요.

No, I have never done it even once.

✎ Work Out 1

Translate the following Korean sentences into English.

1. 그 책을 읽어 본 적이 있어요?

_____

2. 피아노를 한번도 안 쳐 봤어요.

_____

3. 대학교 테니스 코트에서 테니스를 한번 쳐 본 적이 있어요.

_____

4. 태권도 경기를 본 적이 없어서 언제 한번 보고 싶어요.

_____

5. 역 앞에 있는 이탈리아 식당에 자주 가 봤어요.

_____

ANSWER KEY

1. *Have you ever read that book? 2. I have never played the piano even once. 3. I have played tennis at the university tennis court once. 4. I haven't seen a taekwondo match, so I'd like to see one sometime. 5. I have been to the Italian restaurant in front of the station many times.*

⓬ Conversation 2

▶ 12C Conversation 2

Ms. Lopez and Ms. Eun-Young are chatting about their interests and hobbies on their way home from work.

은영: 로페즈 씨, 취미가 있으세요?
로페즈: 네, 그림 그리기를 좋아해요. 그리고 책 읽기도 좋아해서
            일주일에 두 권 쯤 읽어요.

은영: 그러세요, 그림 그리기와 책 읽기요. 로페즈 씨가 그린
          그림들을 언제 보고 싶은데요.
로페즈: 네. 은영 씨는 취미가 있으세요?
은영: 그림은 못 그리지만 사진 찍기를 좋아해요. 주말에는 가끔
          카메라를 가지고 나가요.
로페즈: 그러세요?
은영: 로페즈 씨는 악기를 연주할 수 있으세요?
로페즈: 악기는 연주 못 해요. 지금 플루트 레슨을 받고 있는데
          잘 연주하지는 못해요. 사실은 아주 어려워요. 은영 씨는
          어떠세요?
은영: 바이올린, 첼로, 그리고 피아노를 연주할 수 있어요.
로페즈: 와, 정말 대단하시네요. 바이올린, 첼로, 피아노 중에 어떤 것을
          가장 잘 하세요?
은영: 20년 동안 레슨을 받았기 때문에 바이올린을 가장 잘 연주해요.
로페즈: 그러세요?
은영: 지금 사용하는 바이올린은 낡아서 새 것을 사고 싶은데 너무
          비싸서 살 수 없어요.
로페즈: 콘서트에서 연주해 본 적이 있어요?
은영: 네, 몇 번 해 본 적이 있어요. 사실 이번 주 토요일에 대학로
          레스토랑에서 연주하는데 오지 않으실래요?
로페즈: 그럼요!

Eun-Young:	*Ms. Lopez, do you have any hobbies?*
Lopez:	*Yes, I like painting. And I like reading books, so I read about two books per week.*
Eun-Young:	*Painting and reading books, I see. That's good. I'd like to see the paintings you've done someday.*
Lopez:	*Yes. Ms. Eun-Young, do you have any hobbies?*
Eun-Young:	*I can't paint, but I like taking pictures. On weekends, I often go out with a camera.*
Lopez:	*Is that so?*
Eun-Young:	*Ms. Lopez, can you play any musical instruments?*

Lopez:	*I cannot play any instruments. I am taking flute lessons now, but cannot play it well. In fact, it's very difficult. What about you, Ms. Eun-Young?*
Eun-Young:	*I can play the violin, the cello, and the piano.*
Lopez:	*Wow, that's amazing, isn't it? Which one are you best at: violin, cello, or piano?*
Eun-Young:	*I've been taking lessons for about twenty years, so I'm best at the violin.*
Lopez:	*Is that so?*
Eun-Young:	*Since the violin I am using now is old, I'd like to buy a new one, but it's very expensive, so I cannot buy it.*
Lopez:	*Have you ever performed in a concert?*
Eun-Young:	*Yes, I performed several times. Actually, I will perform at a restaurant in Dae Hak Ro next Saturday, so why don't you come?*
Lopez:	*Sure thing!*

✎ Conversation Practice 2

Fill in the blanks in the following sentences with the missing words. If you're unsure of the answer, listen to the conversation one more time.

1. 책 읽기도 좋아해서_____두 권 쯤 읽어요.

2. 주말에는 가끔 카메라를_____나가요.

3. 지금 플루트 레슨을 받고 있는데_____못해요

4. 지금 사용하는 바이올린은_____새 것을 사고 싶은데 너무 비싸서 살 수 없어요.

5. 사실 이번 주 토요일에 대학로에서_____오지 않으실래요?

ANSWER KEY
1. 일주일에 2. 가지고 3. 잘 연주하지는 4. 낡아서 5. 연주하는데

Grammar Builder 2

12D Grammar Builder 2

RELATIVE CLAUSES

Nouns are usually modified by adjectives, but nouns can also be modified by relative clauses. For instance, in the sentence *The book which I read yesterday is interesting*, "*which I read yesterday*" is a relative clause modifying *the book*.

There are two major differences between the English and the Korean relative clause construction. First, unlike in English, in Korean the relative clause precedes a noun just as adjectives do. Second, there are no relative pronouns (such as English *which*, *who*, *that*, or *whose*) in Korean.

1. Present Tense

Verb all endings + 는

먹다 + 는 = 먹는

앉다 + 는 = 앉는

2. Past Tense

a. Verb ending with a vowel + ㄴ

보다 + ㄴ = 본

가다 + ㄴ = 간

b. Verb ending with a consonant + 은

먹다 + 은 = 먹은

앉다 + 는 = 앉은

어제 본 영화는 아주 재미있었어요.

The movie that we saw yesterday was very good.

작년에 간 여행이 아주 좋았어요.

The traveling that I did last year was very good.

저기서 짜장면을 먹는 사람이 제 오빠예요.
The person who is eating Ja-Jang-Myeon over there is my older brother.

신체가 불편한 사람이 앉는 의자는 노란색이에요.
The chair for those who are disabled is yellow.

어제 먹은 볶음밥은 너무 맛있었어요.
The fried rice that I ate yesterday was so good.

첫번째 줄에 앉은 사람이에요.
It is the person who is sitting in the first row.

When using an adjective to modify the noun in a relative clause, the present and past tense formation are both the same.

Adjective ending with a vowel + ㄴ
예쁜 모자
Adjective ending with a consonant + 은
작은 방

In the past tense relative clause of adjectives, however, the main verb predicates should appear in the past tense.

저는 예쁜 모자가 있어요.
I have a pretty hat.

저는 어제 예쁜 모자를 샀어요.
I bought a pretty hat yesterday.

As you can see, the two adjectives appear in the same tense but the main verb of the second sentence indicates that this sentence is in the past tense.

Unit 3 Lesson 12: Conversations

You can also express the past tense of adjectival relative clauses by using –던.

✎ Work Out 2

A. Use the appropriate forms of the verbs or adjectives given in parentheses to complete the sentences.

1. 이게 제가_____차예요. (원하다)

   This is the car which I want.

2. 스미스 씨가_____사진을 보고 싶습니다. (찍다)

   I want to see pictures that Ms. Smith took.

3. 주말에도_____공원이 있어요? (조용하다)

   Is there a park that is quiet on weekends, too?

4. 플루트를 잘_____친구가 있어요. (연주하다)

   I have a friend who can play the flute very well.

5. 저기서 피아노를_____사람이 존 씨예요. (연주하다)

   The person who is playing the piano there is Mr. John.

B. Translate the following Korean sentences into English.

1. 민준 씨와 같이 이야기 하는 사람은 은영 씨의 오빠예요.

   _____

2. 저는 아버지가 한국 사람이시고 어머니는 미국 사람이신 친구가 있어요.

   _____

3. 주말에 백화점에서 산 스웨터가 좀 비싸요.

_____

4. 작은 부엌이 있는 아파트는 불편한 것 같아요.

_____

5. 주말에 항상 시간이 많이 있는 사람이 있어요?

_____

ANSWER KEY

A. 1. 원하는 2. 찍은 3. 조용한 4. 연주하는 5. 연주하는

B. 1. *The person who is talking with Mr. Min-Joon is Ms. Eun-Young's older brother.* 2. *I have a friend whose father is Korean and mother is American.* 3. *The sweater I bought at the department store on the weekend was a little expensive.* 4. *I think apartments which have small kitchens are inconvenient.* 5. *Are there people who always have a lot of free time on the weekend?*

✎ Drive It Home

A. Fill in the blanks with appropriate words from the word list below.
   해, 적이, 만들어, 있어요

1. 한국에 가 본_____있어요.

   I have been to Korea.

2. 부산에서 사진을 찍은 적이_____.

   I have taken pictures in Busan.

3. 콘서트에서 연주를_____본 적이 있어요.

   I have performed at a concert.

4. 김치를_____본 적이 있어요.

   I have made kimchi.

B. Fill in the blanks with the words in parentheses in their appropriate form.

1. 어제 영화관에서_____영화가 아주 좋았어요. (보다)

   The movie that I saw yesterday was very good.

2. 생선 요리가_____레스토랑에 가고 싶어요. (맛있다)

   I want to go to a restaurant where fish dishes are delicious.

3. 피아노와 바이올린을 잘_____사람이 누구예요? (연주하다)

   Who is the person who is good at the piano and violin?

4. 1월에 생일이_____사람이 몇 명이에요? (있다)

   How many people are there whose birthdays are in January?

ANSWER KEY
A. 1. 적이 2. 있어요 3. 해 4. 만들어
B. 1. 본 2. 맛있는 3. 연주하는 4. 있는

How Did You Do?

Let's see how you did! By now, you should be able to:

☐ talk about past experiences. (Still unsure? Jump back to Grammar Builder 1.)

☐ use relative clauses. (Still unsure? Jump back to Grammar Builder 2.)

Don't forget to practice and reinforce what you've
learned by visiting **www.livinglanguage.com/
languagelab** for flashcards, games, and quizzes!

✎ Word Recall

1. 조개	a. *chance*
2. 주문하다	b. *to give*
3. 기회	c. *shellfish*
4. 새우	d. *to order*
5. 주다	e. *to receive*
6. 한식	f. *shrimp*
7. 받다	g. *salty*
8. 한번	h. *cuttlefish, squid*
9. 짠	i. *Korean-style food*
10. 오징어	j. *once*

ANSWER KEY
1. c; 2. d; 3. a; 4. f; 5. b; 6. i; 7. e; 8. j; 9. g; 10. h

Unit 3 Quiz

Let's put the most essential Korean words and grammar points you've learned so far into practice with a few exercises. It's important to be sure that you've mastered this material before you move on. Score yourself at the end of the unit quiz and see if you need to go back for more practice, or if you're ready to move on to Unit 4.

A. Fill in the blanks with the appropriate question word + particle combination.

1. _____분을 찾으세요?

   Which person are you looking for?

2. _____를 보고 싶어요?

   Who do you want to see?

3. _____못해요.

   I don't do any (of them) well.

B. Fill in the blanks by changing the verbs in the parentheses into nouns with the nominalizer –기.

1. 제 취미는_____입니다.

   My hobby is watching movies.

2. _____는 잘 못해요.

   I'm bad at painting pictures.

C. Fill in the blanks with the verbs in their appropriate form.

1. 한국어 책을_____수 있어요.

   I can read Korean books.

2. 오후 다섯 시에 갈 수_____.

   I could go at 5 p.m.

3. 스페인어를 할 수_____.

   I cannot speak Spanish.

D. Fill in the blanks with the appropriate words.

1. 집이_____좋겠어요.

   I wish the house were big.

2. 피아노를 잘_____좋겠어요.

   I wish I played the piano well.

3. 한국말을 더 잘 했으면_____.

   I wish I spoke Korean better.

E. Translate the following sentences into Korean using the expressions given in parentheses. You'll also need to provide the appropriate particles in order to form complete sentences.

1. *Which is bigger, the U.S. or Korea?* (미국, 한국, 더, 크다)

   _____

2. *The U.S. is bigger than Korea.* (미국, 한국, 더, 크다)

   _____

3. *Among beverages, what do you like best?* (음료수, 중, 뭐, 제일/가장)

   _____

4. *I like coffee best.* (커피, 제일, 좋다)

_____

F. Complete the sentences by using the verbs in parentheses.

1. 서울에 _____ 본 적이 있어요. *(가다)*

   I have been to Seoul.

2. 김치를 _____ 본 적이 있어요. *(만들다)*

   I have made kimchi.

G. Complete the following sentences containing relative clauses.

1. 작년에_____여행이 아주 좋았어요.

   The traveling that I did last year was very good.

2. 어제_____영화는 재미있었어요.

   The movie that I saw yesterday was very good.

3. 피아노를_____사람이 누구예요?

   Who is the person who is playing the piano?

ANSWER KEY
A. 1. 어떤 2. 누구 3. 아무 것도
B. 1. 영화보기 2. 그림 그리기
C. 1. 읽을 2. 있었어요 3. 없어요
D. 1. 크면 2. 치면 3. 좋겠어요
E. 1. 미국하고 한국 중 뭐가 더 커요? 2. 미국이 한국보다 더 커요. 3. 음료수 중 뭐가 가장/제일 좋으세요? 4. 커피가 제일 좋아요.
F. 1. 가 2. 만들어
G. 1. 간 2. 본 3. 연주하는

How Did You Do?

Give yourself a point for every correct answer, then use the following key to tell whether you're ready to move on:

0–7 points: It's probably a good idea to go back through the lesson again. You may be moving too quickly, or there may be too much "down time" between your contact with Korean. Remember that it's better to spend 30 minutes with Korean three or four times a week than it is to spend two or three hours just once a week. Find a pace that's comfortable for you, and spread your contact hours out as much as you can.

8–12 points: You would benefit from a review before moving on. Go back and spend a little more time on the specific points that gave you trouble. Re-read the Grammar Builder sections that were difficult, and do the Work Outs one more time. Don't forget about the online supplemental practice material, either. Go to **www.livinglanguage.com/languagelab** for games and quizzes that will reinforce the material from this unit.

13–17 points: Good job! There are just a few points that you could consider reviewing before moving on. If you haven't worked with the games and quizzes on **www.livinglanguage.com/languagelab**, please give them a try.

18–20 points: Great! You're ready to move on to the next unit.

☐☐ **points**

Unit 4:
Talking about Health

Welcome to the final Unit of *Advanced Korean*. You've come a long way and you should be proud of yourself! In Unit 4, you will learn how to talk about your body and health, speak to a doctor and describe your symptoms when you are sick. By the end of the unit, you'll be able to confidently talk with a doctor about your health and use pronouns where necessary. You'll be able to ask for permission, make negative requests, express obligation, and give advice. Finally, you'll be able to use giving and receiving verbs to express actions done as a favor, as well as describe actions performed in preparation for future events. Are you ready to get started on your final unit?

Lesson 13: Words

In this lesson you'll learn how to:

- ☐ use key vocabulary related to your body and health.
- ☐ use key vocabulary related to visiting a doctor's office.
- ☐ use pronouns.
- ☐ describe actions taken beforehand in preparation for coming events.

Word Builder 1

▶ 13A Word Builder 1

병원	*hospital*

접수대	front desk
진료실	consultation room
대기실	waiting room
진료	medical consultation
초진	the first medical consultation
환자	patient
의료보험 카드	health insurance card
용지	form
몸/신체	body
머리	head
얼굴	face
눈	eye
입	mouth
코	nose
귀	ear
팔	arm
발	foot
다리	leg
가슴	chest
복부	abdomen
허리	waist
심장	heart
뇌	brain
배	stomach
폐	lung
장	intestine
머리카락	hair
통증	pain (aches)

작성하다	to fill in (the chart/paperwork)
부르다	to call (a name)
앉다	to sit down

✎ Word Practice 1

Translate the following words into Korean.

hospital	1.
front desk	2.
waiting room	3.
medical consultation	4.
the first medical consultation	5.
patient	6.
health insurance card	7.
head	8.
eye	9.
mouth	10.

ANSWER KEY
1. 병원 2. 접수대 3. 대기실 4. 진료 5. 초진 6. 환자 7. 의료보험 카드 8. 머리 9. 눈 10. 입

Grammar Builder 1

▶ 13B Grammar Builder 1

PRONOUNS

Let's look at the Korean pronouns corresponding to English *I*, *you*, *he*, *she*, and *it*.

저 (*humble*)/ 나	I
당신	you
그/그분 (*honorific*)	he

그녀/그분 (*honorific*)	she
그것	it

Korean pronouns are not used as frequently as English pronouns. The pronoun 당신 (*you*) in particular is seldom used—such direct address is considered impolite in many contexts, e.g., when speaking to a superior. In fact, when it is used, it is usually with the intention to insult the other person. In all other occasions, the use of the addressee's name or title is more appropriate. Take a look at the following short dialogue between Section Chief Kim and his secretary Ms. Sun-Hee.

선희: 부장님, 내일 미팅에 참석하실 건가요?
Division Manager, are you going to attend tomorrow's meeting?

김 부장: 네, 그래요. 선희 씨도 참석할 거지요?
Yes, I am. Ms. Sun-Hee, you will also attend, right?

선희: 네.
Yes.

그분 is the third person polite form for both a man and a woman. It is also worth noting that pronouns 그 and 그녀 are often used in song lyrics or literary poems. Now, let's look at the plural form of pronouns.

우리/저희 (*humble*)	we
당신들/여러분들 (*addressing an audience*)	you
그들/그분들 (*honorific*)	they (m.)
그녀들/그분들 (*honorific*)	they (f.)
그것들	they (objects)

Both 당신들 and 여러분들 are the plural forms of 당신, but 당신들 is hardly used in daily conversation except in the case when you want to be intentionally impolite. However, unlike 당신들, 여러분들 is often used when you talk to an audience, to refer to multiple listeners. 여러분들 is a gender neutral and can refer to a group of people consisting of both men and women.

The Korean pronouns corresponding to the English possessive pronouns *my, your, his, her, its* are formed by using the possessive marker 의 (*of*).

나의 = 내/저의 = 제 (*humble*)	*my*
당신의	*your*
그의/그분의 (*honorific*)	*his*
그녀의/그분의 (*honorific*)	*her*
그것의	*its*

The Korean indirect object pronouns corresponding to the English pronouns *(to) me, (to) you, (to) him, (to) her, (to) it* are formed by using the indirect object marker 에게.

나에게/저에게 (*humble*)	*(to) me*
당신에게	*(to) you*
그에게/그분에게 (*honorific*)	*(to) him*
그녀에게/그분에게 (*honorific*)	*(to) her*
그것에게	*(to) it*

Finally, the Korean direct object pronouns corresponding to *me, you, him, her, it* are formed by using the direct object marker 을/를.

나를/저를 (*humble*)	*me*
당신을	*you*
그를/그분을 (*honorific*)	*him*
그녀를/그분을 (*honorific*)	*her*
그것을	*it*

✎ Work Out 1

Fill in the blanks with the appropriate pronouns. Don't forget to include particles where necessary.

1. 저기 책상 위에 있는 것이 제 친구 스미스 씨의 카메라예요. _____으로 같이 여행하면서 사진을 많이 찍었어요.

2. 내일 정미 씨와 정미 씨 남편이 같이 오실 거예요. 저도_____과 같이 갈 거예요.

3. 리사 씨와 저는 친구예요._____는 미국에서 만났어요.

4. (showing a picture) 여기 민준 씨가 있네요. 그리고_____옆에 있는 사람이 정미 씨예요.

5. 여기 부장님의 책이 있네요. _____전화해 보세요.

ANSWER KEY
1. 그것 2. 그분들 3. 우리 4. 그분 5. 부장님에게

Word Builder 2

▶ 13C Word Builder 2

열	*fever*
감기	*cold*
두통	*headache*
복통	*stomachache*
메스꺼움	*nausea*
현기증	*dizziness*
설사	*diarrhea*
식욕	*appetite*
수면	*sleep*

알레르기	allergy
혈압	blood pressure
빈혈	anemia
암	cancer
과로	exhaustion from overworking
스트레스	stress
부상	injury
검진	examination
주사	injection, shot
수술	operation, surgery
약	medicine
복용하다	to take medicine
비타민제	vitamin supplement
삼십 팔도	38 degrees
오늘 아침	this morning
심한	terrible, severe
이른	early
적절히	properly
주사를 놓다	to give an injection
수술을 하다	to operate
입원하다	to be hospitalized
퇴원하다	to leave the hospital, to be released from the hospital
열다	to open
닫다	to close
과로하다	to overwork
쉬다	to rest
연락하다	to contact

✎ Word Practice 2

Translate the following words into Korean.

fever	1.
cold	2.
headache	3.
stomachache	4.
nausea	5.
sleep	6.
allergy	7.
blood pressure	8.
anemia	9.
injury	10.

ANSWER KEY
1. 열 2. 감기 3. 두통 4. 복통 5. 메스꺼움 6. 수면 7. 알레르기 8. 혈압 9. 빈혈 10. 부상

Grammar Builder 2

▷ 13D Grammar Builder 2

–어/아야 되다 OR –어/아야 하다 (*HAVE TO*)

When you want to give advice or a warning using *you have to* in Korean—as in *you
have to rest* or *you have to get more sleep*—use the verb followed by –어/아야 되다
or –어/아야 하다. The choice of 어 or 아 depends on the verb's vowel quality.
If the verb has bright vowels such as 아 or 오, use –아야 되다/하다. If the verb
has dark vowels such as 어, 우, 이, use –어야 되다/하다. Let's see some example
sentences with this structure. Don't forget about vowel contraction, and make
sure to use –해요 or –돼요 at the end to be polite.

–어/아야 되다 or –어/아야
하다 (*have to*)

1. BRIGHT VOWELS 1: 아
   가다 (*to go*) → verb stem 가 + 아야 해요 = 가야 해요
   (vowel contraction: ㅏ (가) + ㅏ (아) = 가)

   오늘 동생을 병원에 데리고 가야 해요.
   I'm going to bring my younger sibling to the hospital today.

2. BRIGHT VOWELS 2: 오
   오다 (*to come*) → verb stem 오 + 아야 돼요 = 와야 돼요
   (vowel contraction: 오 + 아 = 와)

   6시까지 집에 와야 돼요.
   I have to come home by 6.

3. DARK VOWELS 1: 이
   쉬다 (*to rest*) → verb stem 쉬 + 어야 해요 = 쉬어야 해요
   (no vowel contraction for dark vowels)

   오늘은 일을 많이 했으니까 내일은 좀 쉬어야 해요.
   I worked a lot today so tomorrow I have to rest.

4. DARK VOWELS 2: 어
   먹다 (*to eat*) → verb stem 먹 + 어야 돼요 = 먹어야 돼요
   (no vowel contraction for dark vowels)

   몸에 좋은 음식을 먹어야 돼요.
   We have to eat food that is good for the body.

✎ Work Out 2

Using the 어/아야 돼요 form of the verbs in parentheses, complete the sentences.

1. 3시까지 병원에 가서 검진을_____. (받다)

   I have to go to the hospital by 3 and receive the examination.

2. 지금 제가 심한 복통이 있어서 빨리 병원에_____. (가다)

   I have to go to the hospital quickly because I have a severe stomachache now.

3. 점심을 먹고 저녁부터는 내일 시험을_____. (공부하다)

   After eating lunch until this evening, I have to study for tomorrow's exam.

4. 과로가 심하니까 3일 동안_____. (쉬다)

   You have overworked severely, so you have to rest for three days.

5. 이 레스토랑은 인기가 많아서 특히 주말에는 꼭 예약을_____. (하다)

   This restaurant is very popular, so we definitely have to make a reservation,

   especially on the weekend.

ANSWER KEY
1. 받아야 돼요 2. 가야 돼요 3. 공부해야 돼요 4. 쉬어야 돼요 5. 해야 돼요

✎ Drive It Home

A. Fill in the blanks with the appropriate pronouns. Don't forget to include a particle where necessary.

1. 존스 씨는 제 친구예요. _____ 사진찍기를 좋아해요.

   Mr. John is my friend. He likes taking pictures.

2. 존 스미스 씨하고_____남동생이 같은 회사에 다녀요.

   Mr. John Smith and his younger brother work at the same company.

3. 내일은 존 스미스 씨의 생일이니까_____ 카메라를 꼭 전해 주세요.

Tomorrow is Mr. John Smith's birthday so please give him the camera.

4. 네, 카메라를 오늘 샀으니까 내일_____ 전해 드리겠습니다.

Yes, I bought a camera today, so I'll give it to him tomorrow.

5. 존 스미스 씨하고 찰스 스미스 씨를 봤어요._____ 형제예요.

I saw Mr. John Smith and Mr. Charles Smith. They are brothers.

B. Fill in the blanks with the appropriate words.

1. 다음 주에 캐나다에_____ 하니까 새 가방을 하나 살 거예요.

I have to go to Canada next week, so I will buy a new bag.

2. 내일 집에서 파티가 있을 거니까 음식하고 음료수를 많이_____ 해요.

There will be a party at home tomorrow, so I have to buy a lot of food and beverages.

3. 내일 친구들과 놀러 갈 거니까 오늘 숙제를_____ 돼요.

I will go out with my friends tomorrow, so I have to do the homework today.

4. 종종 현기증이 있어서 의사를_____ 돼요.

I have occasional dizziness, so I have to see a doctor.

ANSWER KEY
A. 1. 그는/그분은 2. 그의/그분의 3. 그에게/그분에게 4. 그것을 5. 그들은/그분들은
B. 1. 가야 2. 사야 3. 해야 4. 봐야

How Did You Do?

Let's see how you did! By now, you should be able to:

☐ use key vocabulary related to your body and health, and visiting a doctor's office.
(Still unsure? Jump back to Word Builder 1 or Word Builder 2.)

☐ use pronouns. (Still unsure? Jump back to Grammar Builder 1.)

☐ express *have to*. (Still unsure? Jump back to Grammar Builder 2.)

✎ Word Recall

1. 고추		a. *salt*
2. 이사		b. *section chief*
3. 소금		c. *pepper*
4. 설탕		d. *sugar*
5. 사장		e. *regional manager*
6. 조미료		f. *seasoning*
7. 부장		g. *president of a company*
8. 서양식		h. *Western style (food)*
9. 삶은 계란		i. *to drink*
10. 마시다		j. *boiled egg*

ANSWER KEY
1. c; 2. e; 3. a; 4. d; 5. g; 6. f; 7. b; 8. h; 9. j; 10. i

Lesson 14: Phrases

In this lesson you'll learn how to:

☐ enumerate objects and conditions.

☐ use giving and receiving verbs to express actions taken as a favor.

Phrase Builder 1

▶ 14A Phrase Builder 1

두통이 있다	*to have a headache*
복통이 있다	*to have a stomachache*
설사가 나다	*to have diarrhea*
구토가 날 것 같다	*to feel like vomiting*
어지럽다	*to feel dizzy*
심한 현기증이 나다	*to feel extremely dizzy*
오한이 나다	*to have chills*
창백하게 보이다	*to look pale*
의사에게 검진을 받다	*to be checked by a doctor*
병원에서 검진을 받다	*to be checked at a hospital*
주치의에게 상담하다	*to consult a physician*
의사에게 상담해 보시는 게 좋겠습니다.	*You'd better consult a doctor.*
의사와 상담해 봤습니다.	*I have consulted a doctor.*
용지를 작성하다	*to fill out a form*
용지를 가지고 오다	*to bring the form*
처음이다	*it's the first time*
이거면 됩니다.	*It will be okay with this.*
알레르기에 관해서	*concerning (my) allergies*
알레르기에 관한 질문	*questions concerning allergies*
질문에 대한 대답	*answers to questions*
지금 복용하는 약	*the medicine that I'm taking now*
다른 약	*other medicine*
... 이/가 아프다	*... is hurting*
체온을 재다	*to check the body temperature*

미리	beforehand

✎ Phrase Practice 1

Fill in the missing words below.

1. 두통_____있다

   to have a headache

2. _____가 날 것 같다

   to feel like vomiting

3. _____이 나다

   to have chills

4. _____하게 보이다

   to look pale

5. _____에게 상담하다

   to consult a physician

6. _____이다

   it's the first time

7. _____에 관해서

   concerning (my) allergies

8. 다른_____

   other medicine

ANSWER KEY

1. 이 2. 구토 3. 오한 4. 창백 5. 의사 6. 처음 7. 알레르기 8. 약

Grammar Builder 1

▶ 14B Grammar Builder 1

ENUMERATION

In this lesson, we will learn how to list multiple conditions or descriptions in a conversation. First, let's review different methods of enumeration when you are giving a list of nouns or noun class. To enumerate nouns, you have already learned to use –하고 or 와/과 in between nouns. At times, with a longer list, we will use 그리고 (*and*) at the end of the list.

언니하고 남동생
older sister and younger brother

부모님과 남편, 그리고 할아버지와 할머니
parents, husband, grandfather, and grandmother

한국어와 일본어, 그리고 중국어
Korean, Japanese and Chinese languages

In describing conditions with multiple features, you will need to enumerate adjectives or verbs. In this case, we will use the conjunction –고 (*and*).

저는 두통이 있고 배도 아파요.
I have a headache and my stomach also hurts.

여동생이 열이 나고 얼굴도 창백하게 보여요.
My younger sister has a fever and her face looks pale.

When you connect two or more descriptors, the first sentence will drop the sentence ending and take –고 in order to connect with the second sentence. The second sentence will carry the sentence ending. With more than three descriptions, the final part of the sentence will often begin with 또 (*additionally/again*).

영주 씨가 어제부터 어지럽고 구토가 나고 또 심한 두통이 있었어요.
Since yesterday, Ms. Young-Joo has had dizziness, vomiting, and a severe headache.

진섭 씨가 리포트를 끝내고 일을 많이 했고 밤에도 야간 수업을 들었어요.
Mr. Jin-Seop had finished his report and then he worked a lot and took night classes.

누나가 선생님인데 매일 바빠요. 월요일에는 댄스 레슨이 있고 화요일에는 수영 레슨이 있고 수요일에는 학생들과 같이 스터디 그룹 모임이 있어요.
My older sister is a teacher and she is busy every day. Monday she has a dance lesson, Tuesday she has a swimming lesson, and Wednesday she has a study group with her students.

저는 오늘 1시에 점심을 먹고 2시에 수업을 듣고 또 3시에 친구를 만나요.
Today I eat lunch at 1, take a class at 2, and meet my friend at 3.

그 의사가 친절하고 정확한 의사라고 하네요.
I heard that the doctor is a kind and accurate doctor.

오늘 숙제는 짧고 쉬워서 좋습니다.
Today's homework is short and easy, so it is good.

✎ Work Out 1

Fill in the blanks by choosing the appropriate adjective from the list below.

크다, 편리하다, 길다, 높다, 불편하다, 깨끗하다, 좋다, 어렵다, 가깝다, 작다, 친절하다, 오래되다, 지루하다

–어/아야 되다 or –어/아야
하다 (*have to*)

Giving and receiving verbs:
favors

1. 역에서_____고_____아파트에 살고 싶어요.

   I want to live in an apartment which is close to the station and convenient.

2. 선생님이_____고 _____세요.

   That teacher is kind and good.

3. 그 빌딩이_____고_____요.

   That building is small and inconvenient.

4. 이 책이_____고_____고 _____요.

   This book was long, difficult, and boring.

5. 민아 씨 집이_____고 ____고 _____지요?

   Ms. Min-Ah's house is high, big, and clean, isn't it?

ANSWER KEY
1. 가깝, 편리한 2. 친절하, 좋으 3. 작, 불편해 4. 길, 어렵, 지루해 5. 높, 크, 깨끗하

Phrase Builder 2

▶ 14C Phrase Builder 2

감기에 걸리다	*to catch a cold*
열이 있다	*to have a fever*
열을 재다	*to check one's temperature*
목이 붓다	*to have a sore throat*
식욕이 있다	*to have an appetite*
식욕이 없다	*to have no appetite*
고혈압이 있다	*to have high blood pressure*
저혈압이 있다	*to have low blood pressure*
수면을 취하다	*to get some sleep*
불면증으로 고생하다	*to suffer from insomnia*

스트레스가 쌓이다	*to be under stress (lit: stress has accumulated)*
어깨가 결리다	*to have stiff shoulders*
부상 당하다	*to get injured*
골절상을 입다	*to break a bone*
삐다	*to have a sprain*
다섯 시간밖에 못자다	*to have only five hours of sleep*
아는 의사	*the doctor that I know*
연락하다	*to contact*
미리 연락하다	*to contact beforehand*
일찍 집에 가다	*to go home early*
휴식을 취하는 게 좋겠다	*you'd better get some rest*
병가를 내다	*to take sick leave*
과로하지 마세요	*Please don't overwork.*

✎ Phrase Practice 2

Fill in the missing words below.

1. 감기_____걸리다

   to catch a cold

2. 열_____있다

   to have a fever

3. 목_____붓다

   to have a sore throat

4. _____이 있다

   to have an appetite

5. _____이 있다

to have high blood pressure

6. 수면을_____.

to get some sleep

7. 불면증_____고생하다

to suffer from insomnia

8. _____당하다

to get injured

9. _____하지 마세요.

Please don't overwork.

ANSWER KEY
1. 에 2. 이 3. 이 4. 식욕 5. 고혈압 6. 취하다 7. 으로 8. 부상 9. 과로

Grammar Builder 2

▶ 14D Grammar Builder 2

GIVING AND RECEIVING VERBS: FAVORS

When you do someone a favor or receive the benefit of someone else's favor, the grammatical structure will involve different particles depending on the direction of the action.

1. *From A* = A 에게서/A한테서

김종수 씨에게서 책을 받았어요.
I received a book from Mr. Kim Jong-Soo.

순영 씨에게서 크리스마스 카드를 받았어요.
I received a Christmas card from Ms. Soon-Young.

의사 선생님에게서 좋지 않은 말을 들었습니다.
I heard some bad news from the doctor.

어머니한테서 돈을 받았습니다.
I received money from mom.

아버지한테서 작은 소포가 왔습니다.
A small parcel came from father.

2. *To A*: A에게/A한테

친한 친구에게 일주일에 한번 전화를 합니다.
I call my close friend once a week.

일주일 전에 오빠에게 생일 선물을 보냈습니다.
I sent a birthday gift to my older brother a week ago.

요즘은 동생한테 운전하는 것을 가르치고 있습니다.
These days I teach driving to my younger sibling.

형한테 부탁을 하나 하고 싶습니다.
I would like to ask a favor from the older brother.

3. *To A*: A께 (honorific)—used for honorific expressions

부모님께 인사를 드리세요.
Please send a greeting to my parents.

–어/아야 되다 or –어/아야
하다 (*have to*)

Giving and receiving verbs:
favors

선생님께 꽃을 드렸습니다.
I gave flowers to my teacher.

할머니께 점심을 사 드렸습니다.
I bought lunch for my grandmother.

✎ Work Out 2

Choose appropriate particles depending on the direction of the action as well as the politeness of the social situation.
한테, 에게, 에게서, 한테서, 께

1. 윤식 씨가 불고기를 먹고 싶어 해서 제가 내일은 윤식 씨_____불고기를 만들어 주기로 했습니다. (**written**)

   Mr. Yoon-Shik wants to eat some bulgogi so I decided to make bulgogi for him tomorrow.

2. 어제 어머니_____제 두통을 걱정하시는 전화가 왔습니다. (**written**)

   The call came from mother yesterday, worrying about my headache.

3. 이번 여동생의 생일에 우리 형과 함께 여동생_____새 노트북을 사 줄 거예요. (**casual**)

   For this birthday of our younger sister, I and my older brother will buy a new notebook for her.

4. a: 이번 스승의 날에 무슨 선물을 드릴까요?

   b: 김 선생님_____는 빨간 가방을 사 드리세요.

   a: *Which gift should I give on the Teacher Appreciation Day?*

   b: *As for Ms. Kim, buy and give her a red bag.*

5. 민영 씨＿＿＿＿ 파티에 가자는 초대를 받았어요. (casual)

I received an invitation to the party from Mr. Min-Young.

ANSWER KEY
1. 에게 2. 에게서 3. 한테 4. 께 5. 한테서

✎ Drive It Home

A. Fill in the blanks by inserting appropriate connecting words.

1. 저는 두통이 있＿＿＿배도 아파요.

I have a headache and my stomach also hurts.

2. 부모님과 남편＿＿＿＿＿할아버지와 할머니

parents, husband, grandfather, and grandmother

3. 여동생이 열이 나＿＿＿얼굴도 창백하게 보여요.

My younger sister has a fever and her face looks pale.

B. Fill in the blanks by inserting the particles in parentheses appropriate to the direction of the action.

1. 할머니＿＿＿점심을 사 드렸습니다.

I bought lunch for my grandmother.

2. 미선 씨는 부모님＿＿＿매주 토요일마다 전화를 합니다.

Ms. Mi-Sun calls her parents every Saturday.

3. 도서관에서 빌린 책을 미국인 친구 빌 씨＿＿＿＿주었습니다. (written)

I gave the book I borrowed from the library to my American friend Mr. Bill.

4. 한국 친구들＿＿＿인사를 하고 미국으로 돌아가고 싶어요. (casual)

I want to return to the U.S. after I say good-bye to my Korean friends.

5. 어제 제 여자 친구_____정말 멋있는 시계를 받았어요.

I received a really stylish watch from my girlfriend.

ANSWER KEY
A. 1. 고 2. 그리고 3. 고
B. 1. 께 2. 께 3. 에게 4. 한테 5. 한테서

🌐 Culture Note

While Western medicine is widely popular and mainstream, Eastern medicine or various alternative treatments are well received in Korea as well. Some people prefer to have acupuncture when they catch a cold or sprain their ankle. Korea has affordable medical plans for all citizens so when they are sick it is often the case that they can simply walk into the hospital and be treated immediately. Also, some people prefer taking herbal medicines or food supplements depending on their aches; these can be purchased over the counter.

How Did You Do?

Let's see how you did! By now, you should be able to:

☐ enumerate objects and conditions. (Still unsure? Jump back to Grammar Builder 1.)

☐ use giving and receiving verbs to express actions taken as a favor. (Still unsure? Jump back to Grammar Builder 2.)

✏️ Word Recall

1. 운동	a. *price*
2. 취미	b. *book*
3. 가격	c. *next time*
4. 열 병	d. *swimming*
5. 수영	e. *hobby*
6. 다음	f. *exercise(s)*

7. 춥다   g. *ten bottles*

8. 경기   h. *game*

9. 책   i. *to be cold*

ANSWER KEY
1. f; 2. e 3. a; 4. g; 5. d; 6. c; 7. i; 8. h; 9. b; 10. f

Lesson 15: Sentences

In this lesson you'll learn how to:

☐ ask for permission.

☐ make negative requests.

Sentence Builder 1

▶ 15A Sentence Builder 1

의료보험 카드 있으세요?	*Do you have an insurance card? (polite)*
이거 괜찮습니까?	*Is this okay? (deferential)*
예약하셨습니까?	*Did you make an appointment? (deferential)*
예약을 해야 됩니까?	*Do I have to make an appointment? (deferential)*
예약을 안 하셨다면 좀 기다리셔야 돼요.	*If you didn't make an appointment, you have to wait for a little while. (polite [요] and honorific [서])*
어디가 편찮으세요?	*Where does it feel bad (with you)? (polite and honorific)*

두통이 있고 구토가 날 것 같아요.	*I have a headache and feel like vomiting.*
오늘 아침에 어지럽기까지 했어요.	*This morning I felt dizzy, too.*
병원에서 한번 검진을 받는 것이 좋다고 생각했습니다.	*I thought I'd better get checked at a hospital for once. (deferential)*
이 병원 의사에게 검진 받은 적 있으세요?	*Do you have a doctor at this hospital?*
저기 의자에 앉으셔서 이 용지를 작성하신 후 가지고 오세요.	*Please sit down on the chair over there, fill out this form, and bring it back.*
알레르기에 관한 질문에 답을 써 주시겠어요?	*Could you write the answers to the questions concerning allergies? (polite and honorific)*
현재 복용하고 계신 약이 있으시면 그것도 써 주세요.	*If you have any medicine that you are currently taking, please write that, too. (polite and honorific)*
특별한 알레르기는 없는데요.	*I don't have any allergies in particular.*
비타민제는 복용하지만 다른 약은 복용 안 합니다.	*I am taking a vitamin supplement, but I'm not taking any other medicine. (deferential)*
앉아서 기다리시면 이름을 불러 드리겠습니다.	*If you please sit and wait, we will call your name. (deferential)*

✎ Sentence Practice 1

Fill in the missing words in each of the following sentences.

1. _____괜찮습니까?

Is this okay?

2. 두통이 있고_____날 것 같아요.

   I have a headache and feel like vomiting.

3. 병원에서 한번 검진을 받는 것이_____생각했습니다.

   I thought I'd better get checked at a hospital for once.

4. 이 병원 의사에게_____받은 적 있으세요?

   Have you been checked by a doctor at this hospital before?

5. 저기 의자에 앉으셔서 이 용지를_____후 가지고 오세요.

   Please sit down on the chair over there, fill out this form, and bring it back.

6. 현재_____계신 약이 있으시면 그것도 써 주세요.

   If you have any medicine that you are currently taking, please write that, too.

7. 특별한_____ 없는데요.

   I don't have any allergies in particular.

8. 비타민제는_____다른 약은 복용 안 합니다.

   I am taking a vitamin supplement, but I'm not taking any other medicine.

ANSWER KEY
1. 이거 2. 구토가 3. 좋다고 4. 검진 5. 작성하신 6. 복용하고 7. 알레르기는 8. 복용하지만

Grammar Builder 1
▶ 15B Grammar Builder 1

ASKING FOR PERMISSION

You can ask for permission using the following structure.

Verb + –어/아도 됩니까? (deferential)

Verb + –어/아도 돼요? (polite)

여기 앉아도 됩니까?
May I sit down here?
네, 그러세요.
Yes, please.

교수님, 질문해도 됩니까?
Professor, may I ask a question?
네, 그러세요.
Yes, please.

엄마, 이 케익을 먹어도 돼요?
Mom, may I eat this cake?
저녁 먹고 먹는 게 어떠니?
How about you eat it after dinner?

사장님, 이 책 좀 빌려도 됩니까?
President (of the company), may I borrow this book?
네, 그러세요.
Yes, please.

담배 좀 피워도 됩니까?
Do you mind if I smoke?
죄송하지만 여기서는 안 됩니다.
Sorry, but it is forbidden here.

✎ Work Out 1

Construct sentences asking for permission using the words provided in parentheses.

1. 사장님, . . . ? (아픈데, 아내가, 가도, 일찍, 됩니까)

_____

2. 아버지, . . . ? (차, 빌려도, 내일, 좀, 될까요?)

_____

3. 선생님, . . . ? (사무실에, 있는데, 됩니까, 질문이, 오후에, 내일, 가도)

_____

4. 이 방이 너무 더운데 . . . ? (좀, 창문 [*window*], 돼요, 열어도)

_____

5. A: 생일 파티에 정민 씨는 무슨 음식을 먹고 싶어요? B: . . . ? (자장면과 [*noodle dish*], 시켜도, 탕수육을 [*sweet pork*], 돼요)

_____

6. 아침부터 일을 많이 해서 너무 피곤한데 . . . ? (취해도, 휴식을, 돼요?)

_____

ANSWER KEY
1. 아내가 아픈데 일찍 가도 됩니까? 2. 내일 차 좀 빌려도 될까요? 3. 질문이 있는데 내일 오후에 사무실에 가도 됩니까? 4. 창문 좀 열어도 돼요? 5. 자장면과 탕수육을 시켜도 돼요 6. 휴식을 취해도 돼요

Sentence Builder 2

▶ 15C Sentence Builder 2

| 여기 앉으세요. | *Please sit down here.* |
| 두통, 메스꺼움, 그리고 현기증이요? | *A headache, nausea, and dizziness?* |

아직도 어지러우세요?	*Do you still feel dizzy?*
오늘 아침에 심하게 어지러워서 깜짝 놀랐습니다.	*This morning I was extremely dizzy, which startled me.*
체온을 재 볼게요.	*Let's check your temperature.*
삼십 팔도인데 약간 열이 있네요.	*It's thirty-eight degrees, so you have a little fever.*
입을 벌려 보세요.	*Please open your mouth.*
목이 아프세요?	*Do you have a sore throat?*
설사가 있으세요?	*Do you have diarrhea?*
복통은 없고 설사도 안 합니다.	*I don't have a stomachache, and I don't have diarrhea either.*
지금 일 때문에 바빠서 매일 밤 야근을 합니다.	*I am very busy with my work now and am working overtime every night.*
잠은 충분히 주무세요?	*Are you getting enough sleep?*
하루에 다섯 시간밖에 못 잡니다.	*I'm only getting five hours of sleep.*
아마도 과로인 것 같습니다	*Perhaps it's exhaustion.*
한번 검진을 받으셔야겠습니다.	*You'd better get examined for once.*
대학 병원에 제가 아는 의사 선생님이 있는데 미리 연락을 하겠습니다.	*There's a doctor who I know at the university hospital, so I will contact him beforehand.*
오늘은 과로하지 마세요.	*Please don't overwork today.*
일찍 집에 가셔서 좀 쉬셔야 겠습니다.	*You'd better go home early and get some rest.*

✎ Sentence Practice 2

Fill in the missing words in each of the following sentences.

1. 여기_____.

   Please sit down here.

2. 오늘 아침에 심하게_____깜짝 놀랐습니다.

   This morning I was extremely dizzy, which startled me.

3. 체온을_____볼게요.

   Let's check the temperature.

4. 지금 일 때문에 바빠서 매일 밤_____합니다.

   I am very busy with my work now and am working overtime every night.

5. 잠은 충분히_____?

   Are you getting enough sleep?

6. 하루에 다섯_____못 잡니다.

   I'm getting only five hours of sleep.

7. 아마도 과로인 것_____.

   Perhaps it's exhaustion.

8. 일찍 집에 가서서 좀_____겠습니다.

   You'd better go home early and get some rest.

   ANSWER KEY
   1. 앉으세요 2. 어지러워서 3. 재 4. 야근을 5. 주무세요 6. 시간밖에 7. 같습니다 8. 쉬셔야

Grammar Builder 2

(▶) 15D Grammar Builder 2

NEGATIVE REQUESTS

You learned how to make requests in *Intermediate Korean*. Now, let's learn how to make negative requests—as in the English expression *Please don't do that.*

Verb + 지 마십시오 (deferential)
Verb + 지 마세요 (polite)

여기로 들어오지 마십시오.
Please don't enter here.

열이 있으면 목욕을 하지 마십시오.
If you have a fever, please don't take a bath.

이 레스토랑에서 담배를 피우지 마십시오.
Please don't smoke in this restaurant.

미술관에서 사진을 찍지 마세요.
Please don't take pictures in the art museum.

그 컴퓨터를 쓰지 마세요.
Please don't use that computer.

과로하지 마세요.
Please don't overwork.

토요일에는 일하지 마시고 좀 쉬세요.
Please don't work on Saturdays and get some rest.

다른 사람에게 말하지 마세요.
Please don't tell (it to) anyone.

✎ Work Out 2

Make negative requests using the expressions provided in parentheses. You will need to change the verbs to their appropriate form. Use polite endings.

1. 열이 좀 있지만 약을 너무 많이_____. (복용하다)

2. 한 시간 이상 *(more)* _____. (기다리다)

3. 음식이 맛있지만 너무 많이 _____. (드시다)

4. 어제 파티에 가서 술을 많이 마셨으니까 오늘은 너무 많이_____.

   (마시다)

ANSWER KEY
1. 복용하지 마세요 2. 기다리지 마세요 3. 드시지 마세요 4. 마시지 마세요

✎ Drive It Home

A. Fill in the blanks by inserting appropriate expressions given below.
   불러도, 피워도, 복용하셔도, 주무셔도, 앉아도

1. 여기_____ 됩니까?

   May I sit down here?

2. 이 식당에서 담배를_____ 돼요?

   May I smoke in this restaurant?

3. 이 약을 하루에 세 번까지 _____좋습니다.

   It is good to take this medicine up to three times a day.

4. 하루에 일곱 시간 정도 _____ 됩니다.

It is OK if you sleep about seven hours a day.

5. 이름을 _____ 되겠습니까?

May I call you by your name?

B. Fill in the blanks with the appropriate words.

1. 이 레스토랑에서 담배를 피우지 _____.

Please don't smoke in this restaurant.

2. 오후 5시 이후에는 의사에게 _____ 마세요.

Please don't go to the doctor after 5 p.m.

3. 미술관에서 사진을 _____ 마세요.

Please don't take pictures in the art museum.

4. 그 컴퓨터는 _____ 마세요.

Please don't use that computer.

ANSWER KEY
A. 1. 앉아도 2. 피워도 3. 복용하셔도 4. 주무셔도 5. 불러도
B. 1. 마세요 2. 가지 3. 찍지 4. 쓰지

💡 Tip!

Imagine that you are a teacher, flight attendant, policeman, landlord, or superintendent at a museum. Think of some situations where you would ask other people, such as students, customers, drivers, or tenants not to do certain things. Try giving those negative requests in Korean using –지 마세요. You should try forming sentences using words you already know. If you need to use the words that have not been introduced yet, you can always look them up in a dictionary.

How Did You Do?

Let's see how you did! By now, you should be able to:

☐ ask for permission. (Still unsure? Jump back to Grammar Builder 1.)

☐ make negative requests. (Still unsure? Jump back to Grammar Builder 2.)

✎ Word Recall

1. 전부	a. *to play (a musical instrument)*
2. 오징어	b. *all*
3. 연주하다	c. *to drink*
4. 마시다	d. *squid*
5. 공연하다	e. *photograph*
6. 불다	f. *to perform (musical instruments)*
7. 보다	g. *special ability, special skill*
8. 치다	h. *to see, to meet*
9. 특기	i. *to play (a wind instrument)*
10. 사진	j. *to play (piano, guitar)*

ANSWER KEY
1. b; 2. d; 3. a; 4. c; 5. f; 6. i; 7. h; 8. j; 9. g; 10. e

Lesson 16: Conversations

In this lesson you'll learn how to:

☐ express *only* in negation forms.

☐ give advice.

🎧 Conversation 1

▶ 16A Conversation 1

Mr. Shin-Cheol does not feel well, so he is visiting the doctor's office close to his workplace. (접수원 = *receptionist*)

접수원:	성함이 어떻게 되세요?
신철:	박신철입니다.
접수원:	예약하셨어요?
신철:	아니요, 예약을 해야 됩니까?
접수원:	예약을 안 하셨다면 좀 기다리셔야 돼요. 괜찮으시겠어요?
신철:	네, 괜찮습니다.
접수원:	어디가 편찮으세요?
신철:	어제부터 두통이 있고 구토가 날 것 같아요. 오늘 아침에는 현기증도 나고 병원에서 한번 검진을 받는 것이 좋다고 생각했습니다.
접수원:	그러세요? 이전에 이 병원 의사에게 검진 받은 적 있으세요?
신철:	아니요, 처음이에요.
접수원:	그럼 저기 의자에 앉으셔서 이 용지를 작성하신 후 가지고 오세요.

(five minutes later)

신철:	이거 괜찮습니까?
접수원:	네, 그런데 여기 알레르기에 관한 질문에도 답을 써 주시겠어요? 그리고 현재 복용하고 계신 약이 있으시면 그것도 써 주세요.
신철:	특별한 알레르기는 없는데요. 그리고 비타민제는 복용하지만 다른 약은 복용 안 합니다. 비타민제밖에 복용 안 해요.
접수원:	그러세요. 그리고 의료 보험 카드 있으세요?
신철:	네, 여기 있습니다.
접수원:	그럼, 앉아서 기다리시면 이름을 불러 드리겠습니다.
신철:	네.

Receptionist:	*What's your name?*
Shin-Cheol:	*Pak Shin-Cheol.*
Receptionist:	*Did you make an appointment?*
Shin-Cheol:	*No. Do I have to make an appointment?*
Receptionist:	*If you didn't make an appointment, you have to wait for a little while. Is it okay with you?*
Shin-Cheol:	*Yes, it's okay.*
Receptionist:	*Where does it feel bad?*
Shin-Cheol:	*I have a headache since yesterday and also feel like vomiting. I also felt dizzy this morning, so I thought I'd better get checked at a hospital for once.*
Receptionist:	*I see. Have you ever been checked by a doctor at this hospital before?*
Shin-Cheol:	*No, it's my first time.*
Receptionist:	*Then, please have a seat there, fill out this form and bring it back.*

(five minutes later)

Shin-Cheol:	*Is this okay?*
Receptionist:	*Yes, but could you write the answers to the questions concerning allergies here, too? And, if there's any medicine that you are currently taking, please write that, too.*
Shin-Cheol:	*I don't have any allergies in particular. And, I'm taking a vitamin supplement, but I'm not taking any other medicine. I only take a vitamin.*
Receptionist:	*Okay. And, do you have your health insurance card?*
Shin-Cheol:	*Yes, here it is.*
Receptionist:	*Then, if you please sit and wait, we will call your name.*
Shin-Cheol:	*Okay.*

✎ Conversation Practice 1

Fill in the blanks in the following sentences with the missing words. If you're unsure of the answer, listen to the conversation one more time.

1. 예약을 안 하셨다면 좀_____돼요.

   If you didn't make an appointment, you have to wait for a little while.

2. 오늘 아침에는 현기증도_____병원에서 한번_____받는 것이 좋다고 생각했습니다.

   I also felt dizzy this morning, so I thought I'd better get checked at a hospital for once.

3. 이전에 이 병원 의사에게 검진 받은_____있으세요?

   Have you ever been checked by a doctor at this hospital before?

4. 이 용지를_____후 가지고 오세요.

   Please fill out this form and bring it back.

5. 앉아서 기다리시면 이름을_____드리겠습니다.

   If you please sit and wait, we will call your name.

   ANSWER KEY
   1. 기다리셔야 2. 나서, 검진을 3. 적 4. 작성하신 5. 불러

Grammar Builder 1
▶ 16B Grammar Builder 1

EXPRESSING *ONLY* IN NEGATION FORMS

In the above expression 비타민제밖에 복용 안해요. (*I only take vitamins*), the expression "only" in Korean appears with negative grammar안. 밖에 in this case is a particle that means *only* but it has a particular grammatical disposition. It accompanies only negative grammar structure such as 안 (*do not*) or 못 (*cannot*).

Some verbs in Korean which have negative meaning—such as 몰라요 (*to not know*) or 없어요 (*to not have, to not exist*), 재미없어요 (*to not be interesting*)—will be used without negative, the expressions 안 or 못.

저는 집안 일을 요리밖에 안해요.
As for the chores at home, I only cook.

아버지는 일본어를 못하세요. 중국어밖에 못하세요.
My father cannot speak Japanese. He only speaks Chinese.

남편은 독일에서 일을 해요. 그래서 유럽은 독일밖에 여행을 잘 못해요.
My husband works in Germany. So as for Europe, often we can only travel in Germany.

지금 병원에는 김진표 의사 선생님밖에 안 계시는데요.
In the hospital we only have Dr. Kim Jin-Pyo now.

아직 검진밖에 안 받았는데요.
I only received a medical examination at this point.

지금 집에 여동생밖에 없어요.
Now at home, there is only a younger sister.

저는 물리학은 잘 몰라요. 수학밖에 몰라요.
I don't know physics that well. I only know mathematics.

✎ Work Out 1

Translate the following Korean sentences into English.

1. 저는 한국어밖에 못해요.

2. 저는 어머니가 안 계세요. 아버지밖에 없어요.

_____

3. 요리를 세 개밖에 안 했어요.

_____

4. 지금부터 세 시간밖에 없어요.

_____

5. 전화밖에 안 받았어요.

_____

ANSWER KEY

1. *I only speak Korean. 2. I don't have mother. I only have father. 3. I only cooked three dishes. 4. From now on I only have three hours. 5. I only received a phone call.*

🎧 Conversation 2

▶ 16C Conversation 2

Mr. Shin-Cheol enters the examination room.

신철:	안녕하세요?
의사:	네, 여기 앉으세요. 두통, 메스꺼움, 그리고 현기증이 있으세요?
신철:	네.
의사:	아직도 어지러우세요?
신철:	지금은 괜찮은데 오늘 아침에 심하게 어지러워서 깜짝 놀랐습니다.
의사:	그러세요? 체온을 재 볼게요/보겠습니다. 삼십 팔도인데 약간 열이 있네요. 입을 벌려 보세요. 목은 안 아프세요?
신철:	아니요.
의사:	복통은요? 설사가 있으세요?
신철:	아니요, 복통은 없고 설사도 안 합니다.
의사:	그럼 감기는 아닌데요. 직장에서 바쁘세요?

신철:	네, 지금 일 때문에 바빠서 매일 밤 야근을 합니다.
의사:	잠은 충분히 주무세요?
신철:	최근에는 하루에 다섯 시간밖에 못 잡니다.
의사:	알겠습니다. 아마도 과로인것 같습니다. 하지만 한번 검진을 받으셔야 겠습니다.
신철:	검진이요?
의사:	대학 병원에 아는 의사 선생님이 있는데 미리 연락을 하겠습니다. 내일 오후 2시쯤 괜찮으세요?
신철:	네, 괜찮습니다. 오늘은 사무실에 돌아가서 일을 해도 될까요?
의사:	아프지 않으시면 일을 해도 되지만 오늘은 밤까지 일하지 마세요. 일찍 집에 가셔서 좀 쉬셔야 겠습니다.
신철:	네, 그렇게 하겠습니다.

Shin-Cheol:	*Hello, how are you?*
Doctor:	*Yes, please sit down here. You have a headache, nausea, and dizziness?*
Shin-Cheol:	*Yes.*
Doctor:	*Do you still feel dizzy now?*
Shin-Cheol:	*Now, I'm fine, but I felt extremely dizzy this morning, which startled me.*
Doctor:	*I see. Let's check your body temperature. It's thirty-eight degrees, so you have a little fever. Please open your mouth. Your throat doesn't hurt?*
Shin-Cheol:	*No.*
Doctor:	*What about a stomachache? Do you have diarrhea?*
Shin-Cheol:	*No, I don't have a stomachache and don't have diarrhea either.*
Doctor:	*Then, it's not a cold. Are you busy at your work?*
Shin-Cheol:	*Yes, I'm very busy with my work now and working overtime every night.*
Doctor:	*Are you gettomg enough sleep?*
Shin-Cheol:	*Recently, I am only sleeping for about five hours a day.*

Doctor:	I see. Perhaps it's exhaustion. But, you'd better get examined for once.
Shin-Cheol:	An examination?
Doctor:	There's a doctor I know at the university hospital, so I will contact him beforehand. Is around 2:00 p.m. tomorrow okay?
Shin-Cheol:	Yes, that's fine. May I go back to the office and do my work today?
Doctor:	If you don't feel sick, you may work, but please don't work until late (lit: night) today. You'd better go home early and get some rest.
Shin-Cheol:	Okay, I will do so.

✎ Conversation Practice 2

Fill in the blanks in the following sentences with the missing words. If you're unsure of the answer, listen to the conversation one more time.

1. 여기 앉으세요. 두통, 메스꺼움, _____ 현기증이 있으세요?

   Please sit down here. You have a headache, nausea, and dizziness?

2. 삼십 팔도인데 약간_____ 있네요.

   It's thirty-eight degrees, so you have a little fever.

3. 대학 병원에 아는 의사 선생님이 있는데 미리_____하겠습니다.

   There's a doctor I know at the university hospital, so I will contact him beforehand.

4. 오늘은 사무실에 돌아가서 일을_____ 될까요?

   May I go back to the office and do my work today?

5. 일찍 집에 가서서 좀_____겠습니다.

   You'd better go home early and get some rest.

   ANSWER KEY
   1. 그리고 2. 열이 3. 연락을 4. 해도 5. 쉬셔야

Grammar Builder 2

▶ 16D Grammar Builder 2

GIVING ADVICE

When you want to give other people advice (*you'd better … /you should …*), you can use the following structure.

Verb + –어/아야 겠습니다 (deferential)

Verb + –어/아야 겠어요 (polite)

약을 복용하셔야 겠습니다.
You'd better take the medicine.

집에 가서 쉬셔야 겠습니다.
You'd better go home and rest.

종수 씨, 이번 6월까지는 이 프로젝트를 끝내야 겠습니다.
Mr. Jong-Soo, you'd better finish this project by this June.

승미 씨는 공부를 더 해야 겠어요.
Ms. Seung-Mi, you'd better study more.

어머니는 오늘 밤에 요리를 더 만드셔야 겠어요.
Mother had better make more dishes tonight.

제임스 씨는 한국어 책을 더 읽으셔야 겠어요.
Mr. James, you'd better read more Korean books.

When you want to express your own situation with –어/어야 겠어요, it means *I should …* or *I'd better …*

저는 이번 주에 대구에 가야 겠어요.
I should go to Dae-Gu this week.

저는 오늘 그 친구와 만나야 겠어요.
I should meet that friend today.

Similarly, when you want to negate the advice (*you'd better not/you should not*), combine –지 말다 (negative command infinitive) + 어/아야 겠어요 (*would be better*) = –지 말아야 겠어요.

1. Advice directed to the person who receives a respected speech style:
   Verb + –시지 말아야 겠습니다 or –지 마셔야 겠습니다 (deferential, used for someone else with honorific forms)

2. Advice directed to the person who is younger or advice to yourself:
   Verb + –지 말아야 겠어요 (polite, used for yourself or someone who will not receive honorific forms)

   The first three examples below are used in a professional relationship, such as a doctor giving advice to a patient. They are used in a context where you give advice to the person who is a client, older, or of a higher social status. Thus, you use honorific forms.

   내일까지는 일을 하시지 말아야 겠습니다.
   Until tomorrow, you'd better not work.

   수술 전까지는 식사를 하지 마셔야 겠습니다.
   You should not eat meals before the operation.

   오늘은 회사에 가지 마셔야 겠어요.
   You should not go to work (lit: the company) today.

The following examples show how to give advice to someone younger or to yourself. These examples do not involve the subject honorific 시 as the examples above did.

수업에 늦지 말아야 겠어요.
(professor to a student) *You should not be late to class.*

할머니, 토요일에는 가게에서 일을 하지 말아야 겠어요.
Grandmother, I should not work at the store on Saturdays.

9시까지 기차역에 가야 겠어요.
I should go to the train station by 9.

✎ Work Out 2

A. Using the words in parentheses, give advice using Verb + –아/어야 겠습니다.

1. *You'd better attend the meeting.* (참석하시다)

_____

2. *You'd better read more books.* (읽으시다)

_____

3. *You'd better talk with the company president.* (말씀하시다)

_____

4. *You'd better clean the room.* (청소하시다)

_____

5. *You'd better take a rest.* (쉬시다)

_____

B. Use the words in parentheses and the structure Verb + –지 마셔야 겠습니다 to give advice to your client. Don't forget the particles!

1. *You'd better not see that movie.* (영화)

_____

2. *You'd better not be late for company (work).* (늦다)

_____

3. *You'd better not drink coffee too much.* (드시다)

_____

4. *You'd better not exercise today.* (운동하다)

_____

5. *You'd better not spend (use) so much money.* (쓰시다)

_____

ANSWER KEY
A. 1. 미팅에 참석하셔야 겠습니다. 2. 책을 더 읽으셔야 겠습니다. 3. 사장님과 말씀하셔야 겠습니다. 4. 방을 청소하셔야 겠습니다. 5. 쉬셔야 겠습니다.
B. 1. 그 영화를 보지 마셔야 겠습니다. 2. 회사에 늦지 마셔야 겠습니다. 3. 커피를 너무 많이 드시지 마셔야 겠습니다. 4. 오늘은 운동을 하지 마셔야 겠습니다. 5. 돈을 그렇게 많이 쓰시지 마셔야 겠습니다.

✎ Drive It Home

A. Fill in the blanks based on the English translation.

1. 아직 검진_____안 받았는데요.

I only received a medical examination at this point.

2. 지금 집에 여동생밖에_____.

Now at home, there is only a younger sister.

3. _____안 받았어요.

I only received the call.

B. Fill in the blanks with the appropriate words.

1. 약을_____겠어요.

You'd better take medicine.

2. 열이 있으시면 병원에 가_____겠어요.

If you have a fever, you'd better go to a hospital.

3. 질문을 잘 모르시면 선생님께_____겠어요.

If you don't understand the question, you'd better ask questions to a teacher.

C. Fill in the blanks with the appropriate words.

1. 어지러우시면 나가지_____겠어요.

When you feel dizzy, I think that you'd better not go out.

2. 설사가 있으시면 저녁을_____마셔야 겠어요.

If you have diarrhea, I think you'd better not eat dinner.

3. 두통이 있으시면 파티에 가시지 마셔야_____.

If you have a headache, I think you'd better not go to the party.

ANSWER KEY
A. 1. 밖에 2. 없어요 3. 전화밖에
B. 1. 복용하셔야 2. 보셔야 3. 질문하셔야
C. 1. 마셔야 2. 드시지 3. 겠어요.

💡 Tip!

To practice expressing obligation, try making a to-do list every evening for the following day. If you haven't yet learned the verbs you want to use, you can look

Pronouns		Enumeration	
	–어/아야 되다 or –어/아야 하다 (*have to*)		Giving and receiving verbs: favors

them up in a dictionary. If you continue to do this task for a week, you'll probably start to see some repetition of tasks, but that's fine. Practice—and repletion—makes perfect!

How Did You Do?

Let's see how you did! By now, you should be able to:

☐ express *only* in negation forms. (Still unsure? Jump back to Grammar Builder 1.)

☐ give advice. (Still unsure? Jump back to Grammar Builder 2.)

Don't forget to practice and reinforce what you've learned by visiting **www.livinglanguage.com/languagelab** for flashcards, games, and quizzes!

✎ Word Recall

1. 못하다		a. *to be unskillful*	
2. 잘하다		b. *excellent*	
3. 실력이 안 좋은		c. *to do*	
4. 뛰어난		d. *to be bad at*	
5. 하다		e. *to be good at*	
6. 첼로		f. *to swim*	
7. 수영하다		g. *cello*	
8. 수학		h. *reading books*	
9. 악기		i. *math*	
10. 독서/책 읽기		j. *musical instrument*	

ANSWER KEY
1. d; 2. e; 3. a; 4. b; 5. c; 6. g; 7. f; 8. i; 9. j; 10. h

Unit 4 Quiz

Let's put the most essential Korean words and grammar points you've learned so far to practice in a few exercises. Score yourself at the end of the unit quiz and see if you need to go back for more practice.

A. Fill in the blanks with the appropriate pronouns.

1. _____는 오늘 도서관에 같이 공부하러 가요.

   We are going to the library to study together today.

2. 제니퍼 클락 씨는 피아니스트예요. _____콘서트가 내일이에요.

   Ms. Jennifer Clark is a pianist. Her concert is tomorrow.

3. 현주 씨의 남자 친구가 아주 좋은 ____이세요.

   Ms. Hyun-Joo's boyfriend is a very nice person.

B. Fill in the blanks by using the verbs in parentheses.

1. 내일이 어머니 생신이라서 미리 케익을_____. (사다)

   Tomorrow is my mother's birthday, so I have to buy a cake in advance.

2. 레스토랑에 가기 전에 미리 예약을_____해요. (하다)

   Before going to the restaurant, I have to make a reservation in advance.

C. Connect the following nouns or sentences.

1. 언니, 남동생

   older sister and younger brother

   _____

2. 영주 씨가 어지럽다 + 영주 씨가 구토가 나다 + 영주 씨가 두통이 있다

   Ms. Young-Joo has dizziness, vomiting, and a headache.

   _____

D. Fill in the blanks by choosing the appropriate indirect particle from the word list below.

   에게서, 한테서, 께, 한테, 에게

1. 순영 씨_____크리스마스 카드를 받았어요.

2. 일주일 전에 오빠_____생일 선물을 보냈습니다.

3. 부모님_____인사를 드리세요.

4. 할머니_____점심을 사 드렸습니다.

E. Construct sentences asking for permission, using the words provided in parentheses.

1. (질문, 돼요, 하다)

   May I ask a question?

   _____

2. (들어가다, 방, 돼요)

   May I enter your room?

   _____

F. Fill in the blanks by giving the verbs in the parentheses in the appropriate form.

1. 여기서 담배 _____마세요.(피우다)

   Please don't smoke here.

2. _____ 마세요. (과로하다)

   Please don't overwork.

G. Fill in the blanks by choosing the appropriate negation forms from the English cues.

1. 유럽은 독일밖에 여행을 잘_____해요.

   As for Europe, we can only travel in Germany often.

2. 지금 집에 여동생밖에_____.

   Now at home there is only a younger sister.

3. 지금 병원에는 김 선생님밖에_____계시는데요.

   Currently in the hospital, we only have Dr. Kim.

H. Using the words in parentheses, give advice with the expression –시지 말아야 겠습니다 or –어/아야 겠습니다.

1. *You'd better take medicine.* (약을 복용하시다)

   _____

2. *You'd better not buy this car.* (차를 사다)

   _____

ANSWER KEY
A. 1. 우리 2. 그녀의 3. 분
B. 1. 사야 돼요 2. 해야
C. 1. 언니하고 남동생 or 언니와 남동생 2. 영주 씨가 어지럽고 구토가 나고두통이 있어요.
D. 1. 에게서/한테서 2. 에게/한테 3. 께 4. 께
E. 1. 질문 해도 돼요? 2. 방에 들어가도 돼요?
F. 1. 피우지 2. 과로하지

G. 1. 못 2. 없어요 3. 안

H. 1. 약을 복용하셔야 겠습니다. 2. 이 차를 사시지 말아야 겠습니다.

How Did you Do?

Give yourself a point for every correct answer, then use the following key to tell whether you're ready to move on:

0–7 points: It's probably a good idea to go back through the lesson again. You may be moving too quickly, or there may be too much "down time" between your contact with Korean. Remember that it's better to spend 30 minutes with Korean three or four times a week than it is to spend two or three hours just once a week. Find a pace that's comfortable for you, and spread your contact hours out as much as you can.

8–12 points: You would benefit from a review before moving on. Go back and spend a little more time on the specific points that gave you trouble. Reread the Grammar Builder sections that were difficult, and do the Work Outs one more time. Don't forget about the online supplemental practice material. Go to **www. livinglanguage.com/languagelab** for games and quizzes that will reinforce the material from this unit.

13–17 points: Good job! There are just a few points that you might consider reviewing. If you haven't worked with the games and quizzes on **www. livinglanguage.com/languagelab**, please give them a try.

18–20 points: Wow! Congratulations! You made it through the entire program successfully! Don't forget to come back and review as much as you can. This is one of the keys to learning a new language—not just holding it in your short–term memory, but making it stick in your long–term memory. You can always go back to **www.livinglanguage.com/languagelab** for more practice. Best of luck!

 **points**

Pronunciation Guide

The Korean orthographic system is called Hangeul. Sounds are represented by individual jamo (symbols), and the jamo are combined into syllables. Either two or three jamo can be combined to form a single syllable, on rare occasion, four jamo will be combined in one syllable.

The Korean Alphabet

CONSONANTS	VOWELS
ㄱ giyeok	ㅏ a
ㄲ ssanggiyeok	ㅐ ae
ㄴ nieun	ㅑ ya
ㄷ digeut	ㅒ yae
ㄸ ssangdigeut	ㅓ eo
ㄹ rieul	ㅔ e
ㅁ mieum	ㅕ yeo
ㅂ bieup	ㅖ ye
ㅃ ssangbieup	ㅗ o
ㅅ siot	ㅘ wa
ㅆ ssangsiot	ㅙ wae
ㅇ ieung	ㅚ oe
ㅈ jieut	ㅛ yo

CONSONANTS	VOWELS
ㅉ ssangjieut	ㅜ u
ㅊ chieut	ㅝ wo
ㅋ kieuk	ㅞ we
ㅌ tieut	ㅟ wi
ㅍ pieup	ㅠ yu
ㅎ hieut	ㅡ eu
	ㅢ ui
	ㅣ i

Pronunciation

The consonant characters are said to illustrate the position of the tongue, teeth, and lips when pronouncing that particular letter. Notice how the characters for corresponding voiced (ㄷ *d*) and voiceless (ㅌ *t*) consonants are similar in Hangeul. There are several exceptions to pronunciation rules in Korean; pay close attention to the audio portion of this course so that you learn how to pronounce each word carefully.

Consonants

ㄱ	g	like *g* in *go* when between vowels; sometimes like the *k* in *kept*
ㅋ	k	like *k* in *kept*
ㄴ	n	like *n* in *never*

ㄷ	d	like *t* in *stop* when between vowels; sometimes like the *t* in *tip*
ㅌ	t	like *t* in *tip*
ㄹ	r/l	like *l* in *lip*; between vowels, like *r* in *rail*; at the beginning of words, ㄹ is either unpronounced or pronounced as *n*
ㅅ	s	like *s* in *pass*; when followed by ㅣ, like *sh* in *she*
ㅈ	j	like *j* in *jump* when between vowels; sometimes like *ch* in *check*
ㅊ	ch	like *ch* in *check*
ㅁ	m	like *m* in *mother*
ㅂ	b	like *b* in *boy* when between vowels; sometimes like *p* in *pick*
ㅍ	p	like *p* in *pick*

ㅇ	-/-ng	The zero initial is used in syllables that begin with a vowel sound. When it follows a vowel at the end of a syllable, it is pronounced *ng* (ex. 안 = an; 녕 = nyeong)
ㅎ	h	like English h in hot; when appearing after ㄱ, ㄷ, ㅂ, ㅅ, ㅈ, or ㅊ, it is not pronounced, but instead aspirates the following consonant: ㄱ (k), ㄷ (t), ㅂ (p), ㅅ (t), ㅈ (ch), or ㅊ (t)

Double Consonants

ㄲ	gg/kk	like *k* in *kept* but tensed
ㄸ	dd/tt	like *t* in *stop* but tensed
ㅃ	bb/pp	like *p* in *picture* but tensed
ㅆ	ss	like *s* in *spit* but tensed; when followed by ㅣ, somewhere between *sh* in *she* and *c* in *cease*, but tensed
ㅉ	jj	like *j* in *jump* but tensed

Vocalics

PURE VOWELS

ㅗ	o	like English o in so
ㅓ	eo	like the u in cup
ㅏ	a	like the a in father
ㅣ	i	like the ee in feet
ㅜ	u	like the oo in coop
ㅡ	eu	like the i in bid, but pronounced further back in the throat

IOTIZED VOWELS

ㅛ	yo	like English yo in yo-yo
ㅕ	yeo	like the you in young
ㅑ	ya	like the ya in yacht
ㅠ	yu	like the you in youth

DIPHTHONGS

ㅐ	ae	like the e in set
ㅒ	yae	like yet without the t
ㅔ	e	like the a in take
ㅖ	ye	like yay
ㅘ	wa	like the wa in water
ㅙ	wae	like the we in wet
ㅚ	oe	like the oy in boy
ㅝ	wo	like the wha in what

궤	we	like *we* in *weigh*
귀	wi	like the *whea* in *wheat*
긔	ui	similar to *we*

Liaison

Korean has rules of liaison, which state that when certain sounds are combined, some of them will change to become new sounds. This happens in other languages as well; think of the difference in English between *rate* and *rated*: the *t* sound changes to a *d* sound before *–ed*, even though the spelling is unchanged. This is very similar to the Korean rules of liaison, which are as follows:

ㅋ, ㅍ, AND ㅌ

Whenever you see ㅋ (k), ㅍ (p), or ㅌ (t) before ㄹ (l), ㅁ (m), or ㄴ (n) they are pronounced (ng), (m), and (n) respectively. The ㄹ (l), if following any of the three above, also changes to an (n) sound through this liaison.

습 + 니 = 습니
seup + ni = seumni

고맙습니다.
Gomapseumnida.
Thank you.

ㄹ

When ㄹ (l) follows any consonant apart from ㄹ (l) or ㄴ (n), it is pronounced (n). When ㄹ (l) and ㄴ (n) are together in any combination (ㄹ+ㄴ / ㄴ+ㄹ), they are pronounced as (ll).

CONSONANT ENDINGS

Any word ending in a consonant and not followed by a particle will swallow the final consonant. This means that you will begin to pronounce the sound, but not completely pronounce it.

ㅊ (ch), ㅈ (j), ㅅ (s), ㅆ (ss), and ㅎ (h)

When any of these consonants appear at the end of the word, they are swallowed as above, but the beginning of the sound you produce will be the beginning of a (t) sound.

Grammar Summary

1. PARTICLES

PARTICLE	FUNCTION
을/를	Marks an object
이/가	Marks a subject
께서	Marks a subject, used for subject in honorific expression
은/는	Marks a topic
와/과/하고	*and* (between nouns)
어서/아서	*and* (between verb phrases)
지만	*although, but*
도	*too, also,* or *(both …) and*
너무	*too, too much*
의	*of*
에	Marks a location, static and description, or use with the movement verbs as well as time, months, and days
에서	Marks a location, used with action verbs
ㄴ니까?/습니까?	Marks a question
지요	Used to seek agreement, confirming the information
네요	Used for commenting on things
ㅂ니다/습니다	Deferential ending, formal and used in statement (Use 십니다 for honorific subject)
(으)로	Used to indicate *by means of* (transportation or method)
러	Used to express intention

2. NATIVE KOREAN NUMBERS

하나 (adjective: 한)	1
둘 (adjective: 두)	2
셋 (adjective: 세)	3
넷 (adjective: 네)	4
다섯	5
여섯	6
일곱	7
여덟	8
아홉	9
열	10
열하나 (adjective: 열한)	11
열둘 (adjective: 열두)	12
열셋 (adjective: 열세)	13

3. SINO-KOREAN NUMBERS

일	1
이	2
삼	3
사	4
오	5
육	6
칠	7
팔	8
구	9
십	10
십일	11

십이	12
이십	20
삼십	30
사십	40
오십	50
백	100
이백	200
삼백	300
사백	400
오백	500
육백	600
칠백	700
팔백	800
구백	900
천	1000
이천	2000
삼천	3000
사천	4000
오천	5000
육천	6000
칠천	7000
팔천	8000
구천	9000
만	10,000
이만	20,000
삼만	30,000
사만	40,000
오만	50,000

육만	60,000
칠만	70,000
팔만	80,000
구만	90,000
십만	100,000
이십만	200,000
삼십만	300,000
사십만	400,000
오십만	500,000
육십만	600,000
칠십만	700,000
팔십만	800,000
구십만	900,000
백만	1,000,000

4. NUMBERS WITH COUNTERS

	명	권	대	잔	장	자루	마리
	PEOPLE	BOUND OBJECTS	MECHANICAL ITEMS	LIQUID IN CUPS/ GLASSES/ BOWLS	THIN FLAT OBJECTS	LONG CYLINDRICAL OBJECTS	ANIMAL
1	한 명	한 권	한 대	한 잔	한 장	한 자루	한 마리
2	두 명	두 권	두 대	두 잔	두 장	두 자루	두 마리
3	세 명	세 권	세 대	세 잔	세 장	세 자루	세 마리
4	네 명	네 권	네 대	네 잔	네 장	네 자루	네 마리
5	다섯 명	다섯 권	다섯 대	다섯 잔	다섯 장	다섯 자루	다섯 마리
6	여섯 명	여섯 권	여섯 대	여섯 잔	여섯 장	여섯 자루	여섯 마리

	명	권	대	잔	장	자루	마리
	PEOPLE	*BOUND OBJECTS*	*MECHANICAL ITEMS*	*LIQUID IN CUPS/ GLASSES/ BOWLS*	*THIN FLAT OBJECTS*	*LONG CYLINDRICAL OBJECTS*	*ANIMAL*
7	일곱 명	일곱 권	일곱 대	일곱 잔	일곱 장	일곱 자루	일곱 마리
8	여덟 명	여덟 권	여덟 대	여덟 잔	여덟 장	여덟 자루	여덟 마리
9	아홉 명	아홉 권	아홉 대	아홉 잔	아홉 장	아홉 자루	아홉 마리
10	열 명	열 권	열 대	열 잔	열 장	열 자루	열 마리

5. EXPRESSING QUANTITY OF EXISTING ITEMS

A이/가 [number + counter] 있습니다.	*There are [number] A.*

ENUMERATION

CONNECTING NOUNS: A하고 B **or** A 와/과 B

CONNECTING SENTENCES: S1 ... 고 S2

6. QUESTION WORDS

... (이/가 은/는) 언제예요?	*When?*
... (이/가 /은/는) 어디예요?	*Where?*
... (이/가/은/는) 누구예요?	*Who?*
왜?	*Why?*
... (이/가 /은/는) 얼마예요?	*How much?*
몇 + counter 입니까?	*How many?*
... −이/가/(은/는) 뭐예요?	*What? (polite)*
... 이/가 (은/는) 무엇입니까?/ 뭡니까?	*What? (deferential)*

7. TELLING TIME

한시	one o'clock
두시	two o'clock
세시	three o'clock
네시	four o'clock
다섯시	five o'clock
여섯시	six o'clock
일곱시	seven o'clock
여덟시	eight o'clock
아홉시	nine o'clock
열시	ten o'clock
열한시	eleven o'clock
열두시	twelve o'clock

일분	one minute
이분	two minutes
삼분	three minutes
사분	four minutes
오분	five minutes
육분	six minutes
칠분	seven minutes
팔분	eight minutes
구분	nine minutes
십분	ten minutes
삼십분	thirty minutes
반	half past the hour

8. MONTHS

1월, 일월	*January*
2월, 이월	*February*
3월, 삼월	*March*
4월, 사월	*April*
5월, 오월	*May*
6월, 유월	*June*
7월, 칠월	*July*
8월, 팔월	*August*
9월, 구월	*September*
10월, 시월	*October*
11월, 십일월	*November*
12월, 십이월	*December*

9. DAYS

월요일	*Monday*
화요일	*Tuesday*
수요일	*Wednesday*
목요일	*Thursday*
금요일	*Friday*
토요일	*Saturday*
일요일	*Sunday*

10. DATES

일일	*first*
이일	*second*
삼일	*third*

사일	fourth
오일	fifth
육일	sixth
칠일	seventh
팔일	eighth
구일	ninth
십일	tenth

11. DEMONSTRATIVES

이	this (closer to the speaker)
그	that (closer to the addressee)
저	that (far from both the speaker and the addressee)
이게	this thing (with subject particle)
그게	that thing (closer to the addressee, with subject particle)
저게	that thing over there (far from both the speaker and the addressee, with subject particle)
이건	this thing (with topic particle)
그건	that thing (closer to the addressee, with topic particle)
저건	the thing over there (far from both the speaker and the addressee, with topic particle)
이걸	this thing (with object particle)
그걸	that thing (closer to the addressee, with object particle)

저걸	the thing over there (far from both the speaker and the addressee, with object particle)
이 분/이 사람	this person (honorific/non-honorific)
그 분/그 사람	that person (close to the addressee) (honorific/non-honorific)
저 분/저 사람	that person (far from both speaker and listener) (honorific/non-honorific)
어느 분	which one (honorific)
누구	who (non-honorific)
여기	here
거기	there (closer to the addressee)
저기	there over there (far from both the speaker and the addressee)
어디	where

12. INDEFINITE PRONOUNS

	QUESTION WORD	INDEFINITE PRONOUN
누구/누가	who	someone/anyone
뭐 (무엇)	what	something/anything
어디	where	somewhere/anywhere
언제	when	sometime/anytime
아무것	n/a	anything/nothing
아무	n/a	anyone/no one
아무데	n/a	anywhere/nowhere

13. SUBJECT PRONOUNS

나/저 (humble)	I
당신	you

그/그분 (honorific)	he
그녀/그분 (honorific)	she
그것	it
우리/저희 (humble)	we
당신들/여러분들 (addressing an audience)	you (plural)
그들/그분들 (honorific)	they (m.)
그녀들/그분들 (honorific)	they (f.)
그것들	they (objects)

14. POSSESSIVE PRONOUNS

나의 = 내/저의 = 제 (humble)	my
당신의	your
그의/그분의 (honorific)	his
그녀의/그분의 (honorific)	her
그것의	its

15. INDIRECT OBJECT PRONOUNS

나에게/저에게 (humble)	(to) me
당신에게	(to) you
그에게/그분에게 (honorific)	(to) him
그녀에게/그분에게 (honorific)	(to) her
그것에게	(to) it

16. DIRECT OBJECT PRONOUNS

나를/저를 (humble)	me
당신을	you

그를/그분을 (honorific)	*him*
그녀를/그분을 (honorific)	*her*
그것을	*it*

17. VERBS

CONJUGATION OF THE COPULA 이다

	NON-PAST		PAST	
	AFFIRMATIVE	**NEGATIVE**	**AFFIRMATIVE**	**NEGATIVE**
Base Form	이다	이/가 아니다	이었다	이/가 아니었다
Polite Form	이에요	이/가 아니에요	이었어요	이/가 아니었어요
Deferential Form	입니다	이/가 아닙니다	이었습니다	이/가 아니었습니다
Confirming	이지요	이/가 아니지요	이었지요	이/가 아니었지요
Spontaneous Reaction	이네요	이/가 아니네요	이었네요	이/가 아니었네요

18. THE PLAIN FORM OF 있다/없다

NON-PAST		PAST	
AFFIRMATIVE	**NEGATIVE**	**AFFIRMATIVE**	**NEGATIVE**
있어요 (polite)	없어요 (polite)	있었어요 (polite)	없었어요 (polite)
있습니다 (deferential)	없습니다 (deferential)	있었습니다 (deferential)	없었습니다 (deferential)

19. VERB TENSE ENDINGS

ENDING	FUNCTION
–다	Infinitive
–어/아요	Present Tense (polite)
–고 있어요	Present Progressive (polite)
었/았어요	Past Tense (polite)
–ㄴ/은 적이 있어요	Past Experience (polite)
–어/아 본 적이 없어요	Past Attempt (*haven't ever … before*)
–네요	Comment (polite)
–을 거예요	Future/Probability (polite)
–고 있을 거예요	Progressive form of probability (polite)
–ㄹ(을) 거예요	Probability
–ㄹ/을 게요	Willingness (*I will*)
–세요	Polite Request
–어/아 주다	Direct Requests (polite)
–면	Conditional
–면 … **Verb + past tense** (었/았/ㅆ) + ㄹ/을 거예요	Past Tense Conditional
–어/아요	Simple Statement
–고 싶은데요	Indirect Request
–고 싶습니다	Present Desire for formal occasions
–고 싶었어요	Past desire (*wanted to*)
–고 싶지 않았어요/ –기 싫었어요	Past negative desire (*did not want to*)
–ㄹ/을 수 있다	Present Ability (*can*)
–ㄹ/을 수 있었다	Past Ability (*could*)
–ㄹ/을 수 있을 거예요	Future Ability (*will be able to*)
–어/아야 되다 or –어/아야 하다	Obligation (*have to*)
–어/아도 됩니까?	Asking Permission (deferential)

ENDING	FUNCTION
–어/아도 돼요?	Asking Permission (polite)
–지 마십시오	Negative Request (deferential)
–지 마세요	Negative Request (polite)
–어/아야 겠습니다	Suggestions (deferential) (*you'd better*)
–어/아야 겠어요	Suggestions (polite) (*you'd better*)
–시지 말아야 겠습니다 or –지 마셔야 겠습니다	Suggestions (deferential) (*you'd better not*)
–지 말아야 겠어요.	Suggestions (polite) (*you'd better not*)
–게 어때요?	Suggestions (polite) (*Why don't we …*)
–ㄹ/을까요?	Suggestions (polite) (*Shall we …?*)
–ㅂ시다	Suggestions (polite) (*Let's …!*)
–기 전에	*Before …*
–ㄴ/은 후에	*After …*
–밖에	*Only* (with negative verbs)

20. POLITE FORMS OF SOME COMMON VERBS

VERB INFINITIVES	PRESENT TENSE	PAST TENSE
있다 *to have*	있어요	있었어요
없다 *not to have*	없어요	없었어요
이다 *to be/to exist*	이에요	이었어요
아니다 *to not be*	아니에요	아니었어요
먹다 *to eat*	먹어요	먹었어요
가다 *to go*	가요	갔어요

VERB INFINITIVES	PRESENT TENSE	PAST TENSE
오다 *to come*	와요	왔어요
하다 *to do*	해요	했어요
보다 *to see*	봐요	봤어요
읽다 *to read*	읽어요	읽었어요
듣다 *to listen*	들어요	들었어요
자다 *to sleep*	자요	잤어요
공부하다 *to study*	공부해요	공부했어요
배우다 *to learn*	배워요	배웠어요
받다 *to receive*	받아요	받았어요
주다 *to give*	주어요	주었어요
사다 *to buy*	사요	샀어요
운동하다 *to exercise*	운동해요	운동했어요
쓰다 *to use, to write*	써요	썼어요
일하다 *to work*	일해요	일했어요

VERB INFINITIVES	PRESENT TENSE	PAST TENSE
만들다 *to make*	만들어요	만들었어요

21. POLITE ENDING/PAST TENSE/COMMENT

INFINITIVES	POLITE ENDING –어/아요	POLITE PAST TENSE –었/았어요	COMMENT –네요
하얗다 *to be white*	하얘요	하얬어요	하얗네요
까맣다 *to be black*	까매요	까맸어요	까맣네요
파랗다 *to be blue*	파래요	파랬어요	파랗네요
노랗다 *to be yellow*	노래요	노랬어요	노랗네요
빨갛다 *to be red*	빨개요	빨갰어요	빨갛네요

22. THE PRESENT TENSE PROGRESSIVE

VERB INFINITIVE	PRESENT TENSE POLITE FORM	PRESENT PROGRESSIVE POLITE FORM
다니다 *to attend*	다녀요	다니고 있어요
요리하다 *to cook*	요리해요	요리하고 있어요
공부하다 *to study*	공부해요	공부하고 있어요
입학하다 *to enter a school*	입학해요	입학하고 있어요
참석하다 *to attend*	참석해요	참석하고 있어요

VERB INFINITIVE	PRESENT TENSE POLITE FORM	PRESENT PROGRESSIVE POLITE FORM
유학하다 to study abroad	유학해요	유학하고 있어요
오다 to come	와요	오고 있어요
가다 to go	가요	가고 있어요
먹다 to eat	먹어요	먹고 있어요
자다 to sleep	자요	자고 있어요
듣다 to listen to	들어요	듣고 있어요
보다 to see	봐요	보고 있어요
내리다 to get off	내려요	내리고 있어요
타다 to get on	타요	타고 있어요
쉬다 to rest	쉬어요	쉬고 있어요
빨다 to wash clothes	빨아요	빨고 있어요
읽다 to read	읽어요	읽고 있어요
만들다 to make	만들어요	만들고 있어요
주다 to give	줘요	주고 있어요

VERB INFINITIVE	PRESENT TENSE POLITE FORM	PRESENT PROGRESSIVE POLITE FORM
받다 *to receive*	받아요	받고 있어요

23. THE FUTURE PROGRESSIVE

VERB INFINITIVES	FUTURE/PROBABILITY	PROGRESSIVE FORM OF PROBABILITY
먹다 *to eat*	먹을 거예요	먹고 있을 거예요
가다 *to go*	갈 거예요	가고 있을 거예요
공부하다 *to study*	공부할 거예요	공부하고 있을 거예요
졸업하다 *to graduate*	졸업할 거예요	졸업하고 있을 거예요
만들다 *to make*	만들 거예요	만들고 있을 거예요
참석하다 *to attend (a meeting)*	참석할 거예요	참석하고 있을 거예요
다니다 *to attend (school)*	다닐 거예요	다니고 있을 거예요

24. –때: *WHEN-CLAUSE*

–는 때 **PRESENT**	–ㄴ 때 **PAST/ADJECTIVAL USE**	–ㄹ/을 때 **FUTURE**
내가 자려고 하는 때마다 전화가 온다. *Whenever I intend to sleep, the phone rings.*	4월은 봄꽃이 예쁜 때이다. *April is the month that spring flowers are pretty.*	내일 학교에 갈 때 저도 데리고 가 주세요. *When you go to school tomorrow, please bring me too.*

25. *BECOME* + NOUNS: –이/가 되다

저는 3월에 대학생이 되었습니다.	*I became a college student in March.*
영지 씨가 회사원이 되었습니다.	*Ms. Young-ji became a company employee.*
봄이 됐네요.	*It became spring.*

26. *BECOME* + ADJECTIVES: –게 되다

유명하게 되다	*become famous*
잘 하게 되다	*become good at …*
편리하게 되다	*become convenient*

27. STATING REASONS WITH –(으)니까

PRESENT TENSE	PAST TENSE
좀 작으니까 큰 사이즈로 바꿔 주세요. *It is a bit small so please exchange this with a larger size.* 이 스웨터가 가볍고 따뜻하니까 아주 좋네요. *This sweater is light and warm so it is very good.* 그 공원은 깨끗하고 조용하니까 이번 일요일에 가요. *That park is clean and quiet so let's go there this Sunday.*	정미 씨가 A 회사에서도 인기가 많았으니까 B회사에서도 잘 할 거예요. *Ms. Jeong-mi was popular in company A, she will do well in company B also.* 지난 번에는 회색 스웨터를 샀으니까 이번에는 빨간색 스웨터를 사지요? *We bought a gray sweater last time so this time how about buying a red sweater?* 이번 주에 가격이 많이 내렸으니까 쇼핑을 하러 가야 겠네요. *The price went down a lot this week, so we should go shopping.*

28. EXPRESSING OPINION WITH –다고/라고 생각해요 = *I THINK THAT* ...

Present form of verbs/adjectives
(–ㄴ/는) + 다고 생각하다

Present form of copula
이다/아니다 + 라고 생각하다

Future tense
ㄹ/을 거 + 라고 생각하다

Past form of verbs
–ㅆ/었/았 + 다고 생각하다

29. GIVING AND RECEIVING VERBS

to someone: –에게/–한테/–께
마이클에게 책을 줘요.

I give a book to Michael.
동생한테 책을 줘요.

I give a book to my younger sibling.
선생님께 빨리 가 보세요.

Please go to the teacher quickly.
크리스마스에 할아버지께 선물을 드렸습니다.

I gave a gift to grandfather on Christmas.

from someone: –에게서/–한테서/께
어제 어머니에게서/께 스카프를 받았어요.

I received a scarf from mother yesterday.
제 남자친구한테서 초콜렛과 장미를 받았어요.

I received chocolates and roses from my boyfriend.

30. POTENTIAL FORM OF VERBS

CAN DO: PRESENT

VERB + 르/을 수 있다 = *CAN*			
가다	갈 수 있다 *can go*	자다	잘 수 있다 *can sleep*
오다	올 수 있다 *can come*	공부하다	공부할 수 있다 *can study*
치다	칠 수 있다 *can hit/play*	말하다	말할 수 있다 *can speak*
하다	할 수 있다 *can do*	여행하다	여행할 수 있다 *can travel*
먹다	먹을 수 있다 *can eat*	연주하다	연주할 수 있다 *can play musical instrument*
보다	볼 수 있다 *can see*	잘하다	잘할 수 있다 *can do well*
듣다	들을 수 있다 *can hear*	수영하다	수영할 수 있다 *can swim*

CAN DO: PAST

VERB + 르/을 수 있었다 = *COULD*			
가다	갈 수 있었다 *could go*	자다	잘 수 있었다 *could sleep*
오다	올 수 있었다 *could come*	공부하다	공부할 수 있었다 *could study*

VERB + 르/을 수 없었다 = *COULD NOT*			
치다	칠 수 없었다 *could not hit/play*	말하다	말할 수 없었다 *could not speak*

VERB + ㄹ/을 수 없었다 = *COULD NOT*			
하다	할 수 없었다 *could not do*	여행하다	여행할 수 없었다 *could not travel*

CAN DO: FUTURE

VERB + ㄹ/을 수 있을 거예요 = *WILL BE ABLE TO*			
가다	갈 수 있을 거예요 *will be able to go*	자다	잘 수 있을 거예요 *will be able to sleep*
오다	올 수 있을 거예요 *will be able to come*	공부하다	공부할 수 있을 거예요 *will be able to study*

VERB + ㄹ/을 수 없을 거예요 = *WILL NOT BE ABLE TO*			
치다	칠 수 없을 거예요 *will not be able to hit/play*	말하다	말할 수 없을 거예요 *will not be able to speak*
하다	할 수 없을 거예요 *will not be able to do*	여행하다	여행할 수 없을 거예요 *will not be able to travel*

31. *I WISH ...* = –(으)면 좋겠어요:

집이 컸으면 좋겠어요.
I wish the home was big.
케일이 맛있었으면 좋겠어요.
I wish the case was delicious.

32. RELATIVE CLAUSES

1. Verb ending with a Vowel + ㄴ = action is performed, past tense

2. Verb ending with a consonant + 는 = present tense

3. Verb ending with a consonant + 은 = past tense

33. GIVING AND RECEIVING VERBS

From A = A 에게서/A 한테서
To A: A에게/A 한테
To A: A께 (honorific)

34. CREATING NOUNS FROM VERBS: NOMINALIZER –기 OR –ㅁ/음

Plain form of verbs + –기 OR –ㅁ/음

35. ADJECTIVAL MODIFICATION –은

작은 스웨터	small sweater
좁은 방	cramped room
적은 양	small quantity
낮은 언덕	low hill
넓은 바다	large sea
많은 사람	many people
높은 지위	high status
좋은 도시	good city

36. ADJECTIVAL MODIFICATION –ㄴ

큰 책상	big desk
예쁜 꽃	pretty flower

나쁜 의자	bad chair
친절한 학생	kind student
불친절한 병원	unkind hospital
편리한 시설	convenient facilities
불편한 계단	inconvenient stair
조용한 성격	quiet personality
못생긴 아이	ugly kid

37. ADJECTIVAL MODIFICATION –는

재미있는 친구	interesting friend
재미없는 영화	boring movie
맛있는 음식	delicious food
맛없는 음식점	not delicious restaurant

38. ADJECTIVAL MODIFICATION –ㅂ → –ㅜ

가까운 집	nearby house
쉬운 문제	easy problem
어려운 시험	difficult exam
시끄러운 교실	noisy classroom

39. ADJECTIVES: PAST TENSE

PRESENT	PAST	PRESENT	PAST
무거운 *heavy*	무거웠던	가벼운 *light*	가벼웠던
긴 *long*	길었던	짧은 *short*	짧았던
넉넉한 *a little big*	넉넉했던	좁은 *narrow*	좁았던

PRESENT	PAST	PRESENT	PAST
더운 *warm (weather)*	더웠던	추운 *cold (weather)*	추웠던
따뜻한 *warm (object)*	따뜻했던	찬 *cold (object)*	차가웠던
어두운 *dark*	어두웠던	밝은 *bright*	밝았던
맛있는 *delicious*	맛있었던	맛없는 *not tasty*	맛없었던
하얀 *white*	하얬던	까만 *black*	까맸던
깨끗한 *clean*	깨끗했던	조용한 *quite*	조용했던
활발한 *lively*	활발했던	유명한 *famous*	유명했던
비싼 *expensive*	비쌌던	싼 *cheap*	쌌던
편리한 *convenient*	편리했던	불편한 *inconvenient*	불편했던
좋은 *good*	좋았던	나쁜 *bad*	나빴던
시원한 *cool*	시원했던	부족한 *insufficient*	부족했던
매운 *spicy*	매웠던	짠 *salty*	짰던
재미있는 *interesting*	재미있었던	재미없는 *uninteresting*	재미없었던
친절한 *kind*	친절했던	불친절한 *unkind*	불친절했던

40. ADJECTIVES: CHANGE –어/아 지다

비싸지다	to become expensive	싸지다	to become inexpensive
커지다	to become big	작아지다	to become small (size)
더워지다	to become hot	추워지다	to become cold
많아지다	to become many/ much	적어지다	to become small (quantity)
뜨거워지다	to become hot (to the touch)	차가워지다	to become cold (to touch)
가벼워지다	to become light	무거워지다	to become heavy
높아지다	to become high	낮아지다	to become low
젊어지다	to become young (person)	낡아지다	to become old (goods)
밝아지다	to become bright	어두워지다	to become dark
재미있어지다	to become interesting	재미없어지다	to become uninteresting
따뜻해지다	to become warm	흐려지다	to become cloudy

41. COMPARATIVES

A 이/가 B 보다 더 X	A is more X than B.
A 하고 B 중 뭐가 더 X?	Which is more X, A or B?

42. SUPERLATIVE

A, B, C 중에 A	A among A, B, and C.
D 중에 A	Among D, A
제일 잘 해요	I do/play the best

43. HONORIFICS

HONORIFIC VERBS

BASE FORM	HONORIFIC FORM
먹다 *to eat*	드시다 *to eat food or to drink*
먹다 *to eat*	잡수시다 *to eat a meal*
자다 *to sleep*	주무시다
죽다 *to die*	돌아가시다
있다 *to be/to stay*	계시다
말하다 *to speak*	말씀하시다

SUBJECT HONORIFIC 시

BASE FORM	HONORIFIC FORM
보다 *to see*	보시다
만나다 *to meet*	만나시다
주다 *to give*	주시다
가다 *to go*	가시다
오다 *to come*	오시다

BASE FORM	HONORIFIC FORM
읽다 to read	읽으시다
이다 to be	이시다

HONORIFIC NOUNS

BASE FORM	HONORIFIC FORM
나이 age	연세
딸 daughter	따님
이름 name	성함
사람/명 person, people	분
생일 birthday	생신
집 home, house	댁
밥 rice, meal	진지
말 words, speech	말씀